Innovative School Leadership

Written by school leaders, for school leaders, this book shares the work of ten practising, innovative school leaders. It offers insight into practical school developments that have been researched, trialled and reviewed to demonstrate their success at creating positive change.

With each chapter written by experienced school leaders working in a range of contexts, the accounts of the developments they carried out and the research evidence they collected to measure impact are presented accessibly and succinctly. These developments include:

- 'Poverty Proofing' by breaking down barriers to disadvantage
- Creating a new holistic approach to appraisal and quality assurance
- Designing and delivering a new cohesive whole school curriculum
- Surviving headteacher stress.

Innovative School Leadership: Transforming Practices is an indispensable resource for all current and aspiring leaders wanting to provide the best learning environment for their whole school community.

Gill Richards is Emeritus Professor of Special Education, Equity and Inclusion at Nottingham Trent University, UK.

Chris Wheatley is CEO of the Flying High Trust, an education Trust of over 30 schools in the East Midlands, UK.

A View into the Classroom
Series edited by Gill Richards

A View into the Classroom is a unique series, written by and for education practitioners. Supported throughout with real-life case studies of success, books in this series offer easy access to practical school-based education research for a wide range of teachers who want to understand more about issues that interest and challenge them. With the current focus on 'evidence-based practice' in education settings, all teachers increasingly need to become 'research literate', so these accounts will provide valuable insight for any teacher about manageable research processes that can be incorporated into their own professional activities to become more effective in the classroom, with greater impact on their students.

Effective Interventions and Strategies for Pupils with SEND
Using Evidence-Based Methods for Maximum Impact
Gill Richards and Jane Starbuck

Reducing Teachers' Marking Workload and Developing Pupils' Learning
How to Create More Impact with Less Marking
Gill Richards and Rhian Richardson

Innovative School Leadership
Transforming Practices
Edited by Gill Richards and Chris Wheatley

For more information about this series, please visit: https://www.routledge.com/A-View-into-the-Classroom/book-series/VCLSRM

Innovative School Leadership

Transforming Practices

Edited by Gill Richards
and Chris Wheatley

Routledge
Taylor & Francis Group
LONDON AND NEW YORK

First edition published 2022
by Routledge
2 Park Square, Milton Park, Abingdon, Oxon, OX14 4RN

and by Routledge
605 Third Avenue, New York, NY 10158

Routledge is an imprint of the Taylor & Francis Group, an informa business

© 2022 selection and editorial matter, Gill Richards and Chris Wheatley; individual chapters, the contributors

The right of Gill Richards and Chris Wheatley to be identified as the authors of the editorial material, and of the authors for their individual chapters, has been asserted in accordance with sections 77 and 78 of the Copyright, Designs and Patents Act 1988.

All rights reserved. No part of this book may be reprinted or reproduced or utilised in any form or by any electronic, mechanical, or other means, now known or hereafter invented, including photocopying and recording, or in any information storage or retrieval system, without permission in writing from the publishers.

Trademark notice: Product or corporate names may be trademarks or registered trademarks, and are used only for identification and explanation without intent to infringe.

British Library Cataloguing-in-Publication Data
A catalogue record for this book is available from the British Library

Library of Congress Cataloging-in-Publication Data
Names: Richards, Gill, editor. | Wheatley, Chris (CEO), editor.
Title: Innovative school leadership : transforming practices / edited by Gill Richards and Chris Wheatley.
Description: First edition. | Abingdon, Oxon ; New York, NY : Routledge, 2022. | Series: A view into the classroom | Includes bibliographical references and index.
Identifiers: LCCN 2021019998 | ISBN 9780367612153 (hardback) | ISBN 9780367612160 (paperback) | ISBN 9781003104698 (ebook)
Subjects: LCSH: Educational leadership. | Educational innovations.
Classification: LCC LB2806 .I495 2022 | DDC 371.2—dc23
LC record available at https://lccn.loc.gov/2021019998

ISBN: 978-0-367-61215-3 (hbk)
ISBN: 978-0-367-61216-0 (pbk)
ISBN: 978-1-003-10469-8 (ebk)

DOI: 10.4324/9781003104698

Typeset in Sabon
by Apex CoVantage, LLC

Contents

Acknowledgements vii
Author biographies viii

Introduction 1
CHRIS WHEATLEY AND GILL RICHARDS

1 "An overwhelming, scrutinised, roller coaster experience – I love it!": new headteachers' first 100 days 11
DAVID S STEWART

2 Bottom of the pile? How does it feel to go to the least desirable school in the area? 22
DAVID ANDERSON

3 Avoiding headteacher stress 36
JAMES BROWN

4 Appraisal and quality assurance – a deeper deep dive: a holistic approach to changing the culture of performance management 47
JAMES HUTCHINSON

5 Developing whole-school research 64
MICHAEL GORTON

6 What are you waiting for? Get your school Poverty
   Proofed: breaking the cycle of disadvantage   76
   CHRIS WARDLE

7 School exclusion – just a holiday? What can schools
   learn from experiences of internal and fixed-term
   exclusion?   89
   MATTHEW SAMMY

8 Schools' charity work – who benefits?   102
   LEANNE MITCHELL

9 Creating a whole-school curriculum   115
   LAURA WOOKEY

10 How to improve outcomes for pupils with SEND   129
   EMILY WALKER

   Index   145

Acknowledgements

We especially thank all the contributors to this book for their generosity in sharing their findings and learning.

We would also like to thank all of the staff, students and consultants who contributed towards the school development work carried out by the authors of this book. We hope that their support and experiences will inspire other school leaders and those aspiring to leadership roles, to encourage research-informed innovation practices that will benefit our education community.

We would like to thank Dr Gill Scott for her enthusiastic support of teachers' research when she was Dean of the School of Education at Nottingham Trent University. Her encouragement of innovative outreach work with schools led to Gill supporting teachers' research development and becoming the university's link partner for Inspiring Leaders' National Programme Qualifications courses. It was through this that Gill and Chris met – creating a partnership that jointly supported several research projects within the Flying High Trust and the decision to edit this book.

We would also like to thank Alison Foyle (Senior Publisher) for her continued encouragement of this new venture with publishing teachers' research and the team at Routledge for their support in ensuring that our book was ready for publication.

Author biographies

Editors

Gill Richards is Emeritus Professor of Special Education, Equity and Inclusion at Nottingham Trent University. Prior to this, she taught in mainstream and special schools for 21 years. She has been a project leader for government-funded SEN projects in schools and a European Erasmus project on behaviour management for teachers in Greece. Her recent research includes a NCTL schools-based project on lessening teachers' workload, a project on the impact of teachers' action research in schools, and an eight-year study of the aspirations and achievements of girls living in an area of severe deprivation. She is committed to making research more accessible to practitioners and ensuring that learning from the 'voice' of those taking part in research studies is heard and impacts everyday practice. She currently teaches on the National Award for SENCOs and supports schools in developing their own research culture. She also carries out consultancy work on course development with universities in the UK and internationally.

Chris Wheatley (OBE) is the CEO and founder of the Flying High Trust, an education Trust of 30 primary schools based in the East Midlands. Previously he was headteacher of two schools, leading both on an improvement journey to 'Outstanding.' He became a National Leader of Education in 2010 and co-created Inspiring Leaders (a leadership development group that delivers all levels of the National Professional Qualification for Leadership). He became a director of Inspiring Leaders' SCITT (initial teacher training) in 2015, which received an 'Outstanding' judgement by Ofsted (2018). He secured a position on the National Teaching

School Council in 2015, a role in which he has supported government policy development. He was inducted as a fellow of the Charter College of Teaching in 2019 and received an OBE in the 2020 Queen's New Year Honours List for his services to education. His Trust was awarded Teaching School Hub status in 2021 with the objective to support teacher and leadership development.

Authors

David Anderson is Deputy Principal with a teaching and learning focus at a community college, 11–16 school in the East Midlands. He worked initially as a science teacher in a purpose-built school incorporating special school students into a mainstream setting in East Sussex. He then worked in a large North London school where he became Head of Science before moving to his present school where he progressed to senior leadership. He is passionate about equity in education and is driven by raising awareness amongst teachers and school leaders.

James Brown has been working in schools since 2007, starting in Nottingham City and moving to work in Leicestershire since 2013. James's work has been focussed on developing educational partnerships. These range from working with children and families in local communities to working with teachers and school leaders, and coordinating school improvement activity. James has helped establish a cohort-one Teaching School Alliance, has a senior leadership role in a Multi-Academy Trust and leads a school-based initial teacher training partnership (SCITT). James has experience working with school and MAT leaders, teachers, support staff and colleagues from the private and voluntary sector, and he is deeply passionate about professional development, coaching and organisational leadership.

Michael Gorton has been a primary school teacher since 2012. After completing his PGCE at the University of Leicester he returned to Nottingham and has since taught across the Primary age ranges, from Foundation to Year 5. Over this period, he has engaged with several research projects covering topics like behaviour management and metacognition as part of his interest in educational research. Michael has been maths lead for his school since 2018 and, before his move to Early Years, was the

Phase Leader for Key Stage 1. He now teaches in Foundation Stage, is a member of the school's middle leadership team and is currently completing an MA in education and his National Professional Qualification for Senior Leadership.

James Hutchinson began his career teaching in the late 1990s in the special education sector. He taught across two special schools and three secondary mainstream schools, working in physical education and leadership before becoming headteacher in a medium-sized special school in the East Midlands. James has a particular interest in teaching and learning and systems leadership. He is passionate about collaboration across the sectors and believes that teachers working and learning together is one of the most powerful tools to improve outcomes.

Leanne Mitchell has been a secondary school drama teacher since 1998. She has been Director of Drama at her present school for the past 20 years. Leanne is passionate about students' development outside of the classroom. In her role she has produced many musicals and shows and taken hundreds of students on performing arts tours to Europe. Leanne has also taken students further afield to Africa and Indonesia, working alongside local people on different projects. Leanne is a trustee of a preschool in Kenya and travels there regularly to support the school.

Matthew Sammy is a senior leader at an 'Outstanding' secondary school with responsibility for behaviour and safeguarding. Prior to becoming a senior leader, Matthew held the position of Director of Music, overseeing both curricular and extra-curricular music provision. Matthew is a qualified school inspector and commenced as a contracted inspector in 2013, when he also completed the academic Professional Qualification for School Inspectors (PQSI). Matthew holds a MA in education and is an active member of ASCL's (Association of School College Leaders) BAME networking group.

David S Stewart, OBE, D.Litt.h.c., was a teacher for 43 years of pupils with severe learning disabilities, 27 as a headteacher in Nottingham. During that time the school achieved six 'Outstanding' Ofsted reports. Now retired, he is still a governor for several schools. David has written widely on the history of special education. He has a national reputation for training in the areas of RSE and pupils with SEND. For 30 years, he was the director of the award-winning Nottingham Youth Theatre Inclusive Company. David still works with Nottingham Trent University and the University of Nottingham and is an honorary doctor of the latter. In 2018 he won the One Dance UK Award for most supportive school leader for dance. He is a deputy lieutenant of Nottinghamshire.

Emily Walker has worked in education since 1996, teaching in both mainstream and special schools. She has held various leadership roles, from subject leader to leading teaching and learning, curriculum, assessment and mentoring early career teachers. More recently, Emily has focussed on working with learners with special educational needs, initially as an assistant headteacher in a special secondary school and then as director of a teaching school in the East Midlands which specialises in SEND. She was recently appointed as Deputy Regional Lead for Whole School SEND, representing East Midlands, South Yorkshire and Humber. Emily strongly believes all children deserve the best possible chance to succeed in life and is passionate about supporting teachers and leaders in making this happen.

Chris Wardle has worked in Blackpool schools since 2001. He has worked in four Blackpool high schools as a teacher of science to children aged 11–16. Chris has been a KS3 leader of science, head of science and an advanced skills teacher of science. He then became an assistant headteacher, deputy headteacher and associate principal. Chris now leads in an amazing secondary Church school, a school which has demonstrated rapid and sustained cultural change over three years, leading to improved outcomes for all pupils including those who are disadvantaged.

Laura Wookey has been a primary school teacher since 2004, working predominantly in a junior school in Year 6. Here she became an advanced skills teacher for the local authority and subsequently assistant headteacher with the responsibility for teaching and learning. Laura is now employed by her school's Trust as Lead Practitioner for Teaching and Learning and has additionally assumed responsibility for the curriculum. She still teaches in one of the Trust schools for part of the week to ensure her practice is current. She is passionate about working with staff across the MAT to provide the best opportunities for the children across the group of schools.

Introduction

Chris Wheatley and Gill Richards

An experienced headteacher's view

Why I wanted to do this book

"If only I knew then what I know now..."

After over 20 years in school leadership, two headships and several years as CEO of a large Education Trust, I have found myself reflecting on my experiences as a guide on what to do or not to do when faced with certain situations. Throughout my career I have used any experience I have gained to either support future thinking and developments or to enable me to change strategic direction. It is for this reason that I wanted to be involved in this book. The opportunity for school leaders to pick up this book, search the relevant chapters and reflect on real-life accounts of practice, current thinking, findings and learning, and use this to support or challenge their own thinking is so beneficial and such an opportunity.

Over recent years, schools have become increasingly high-stakes environments. External scrutiny and evaluation and stakeholder accountability have made leadership a role in which mistakes and misjudgements are to be avoided at all costs. Leadership impact and school improvement acceleration are an expectation for all leaders. Schools are increasingly asked to be accountable for continuing progress, providing evidence of impact, value for money and overall effectiveness. This has placed great pressure on all school leaders to make a difference and to positively effect change throughout school operations. With these pressures in mind, there has been a reluctance for many school leaders to innovate, forge an untested path or simply make decisions without the need to consult a risk

DOI: 10.4324/9781003104698-1

register – even though the leader may feel this would make a huge difference – due to fear of scrutiny or uncertainty of immediate impact. This means that leaders have to evaluate decisions by balancing short-term results against long-term, lasting cultural change. Therefore, help and guidance are much needed in this area.

Impact of research

It could be said that 'trail blazer' heads are not celebrated in education as they once were. The term *maverick leader* has taken on a negative connotation, suggesting non-compliance and risk-taking. The expectation for leadership is the ability to make decisions which are primarily research-based, bringing clarity and rationale to any staff team, governor body or any external scrutiniser who needs convincing as to why this is an appropriate course of action to take. So, for a school leader to make decisions or choose a direction of travel for a school is incredibly difficult, particularly if research is thin in this area – which is where this book comes in, providing real learning about real school issues and situations from real leaders. I believe the value of this book is in its authenticity, its actual accounts of practice from current school leaders. I hope leaders and practitioners reading this will access helpful insight on how to overcome some significant leadership challenges, as well as find many innovative approaches to current school practices, enabling them to lead with confidence.

I also hope leaders reading this will reflect on the accounts, try them, learn from them and add their learning to the rich tapestry of leadership research that is so needed for our profession to thrive.

We owe it to our future leaders.

Chris Wheatley

Quality assurance: school leaders *need* researched evidence

Research-informed decisions lead to evidence-based practice

School leaders are used to operating in a world where 'evidence' is expected to 'prove' successful school practice. Increased delegated powers brought increased accountability. Leaders now need to anticipate where an evidence trail *might* be needed and plan processes for the 'just-in-case' situations. The ever-changing education landscape also requires them to engage knowledgably with new expectations as swiftly as they arise.

Deep understanding and application of robust ways to collect evidence ensure that any school claim can be seen to be authentic and withstand tests of scrutiny from external sources like Ofsted and parents or internal groups like teachers and students. This evidence can be wide-ranging – about student attainment, HR processes, 'value-for-money', selection of school equipment, parent complaints, or new teaching and learning initiatives.

'Research' can be viewed with mixed feelings by school leaders. It is easy to see the benefits of using research methods to collect information required about the school or to learn about a new education initiative, but published 'academic' research may be viewed as inaccessible – either to obtain or to read – or difficult to apply within their own unique school situation. School leaders may also be influenced by previous experiences with research, considering some forms of evidence collection as more reliable – like numerical data rather than student 'voice' – or favour particular sources because they align with personal and professional beliefs.

However 'research' is viewed and utilised, and whether this involves active methods to collect and analyse information within their own schools or learning from others' research studies, school leaders need to ensure that decisions are made on robust evidence. Leading a school where staff (and students) are research-literate will enable an enquiring and dynamic environment where processes, practices, developments, targeted strategies and decisions are trusted and assured of their quality.

Why is it important to lead a research-active school?

Making a difference at individual school level

School leaders and their staff are immersed in the life of a school. They have 'insider' knowledge and understanding that can enrich research investigations. With so much spent on education resources to enhance young people's education experiences, getting it right matters. As Hattie (2016) argues, teachers need to determine what works and what doesn't – and more importantly, to know *why* something does or doesn't work. This is the place where many schools start their research and make a difference within their own context.

There can be criticism about practitioner research, because it may be seen as small-scale, anecdotal and non-replicable. I would challenge this view (as do others like Jones 2018; Nelson and O'Beirne 2014), because although there is much to learn from large national/international studies, I think that smaller-scale research helps deepen understanding and relevance at a local level: it offers an opportunity to improve specific school practice and target students' educational experiences.

Schools' engagement with research is also important because:

- An evidence-based approach, underpinned by research, increases informed decision-making. This supports the selection and maintenance of practices with positive outcomes and discards those with negative outcomes.
- It supports 'disciplined' decision-making that examines claims and compares different standpoints, using the best available evidence from multiple, reliable sources.
- It moves from 'quick-fix' solutions by 'heroic problem solvers' (Jones 2018) to leadership that supports facilitation of genuine, shared problem-solving.
- If any unexpected demands for evidence are required, a high-quality evidence trail is already available and easily located.
- Evidence-informed leaders can protect their schools from education 'fads' that make great claims, but waste time and money and do not impact positively on outcomes. Evidence-informed decisions prevent selection of strategies where the cause of lack of success may be placed on students rather than the quality of the strategy, increasing their experiences of failure.
- A lack of engagement will disadvantage the sector because

  - The breadth of published research evidence available will still not reach those who could benefit from it. Researchers have different priorities and produce conflicting results. These may not be clear when studies are disseminated to schools. Without this knowledge, it is hard for busy staff to make informed decisions.
  - Professional researchers will continue to dominate education research, and their results, which may exclude the deeper 'insider' perspectives of teachers and students, will continue to inform national policy.

Tried and tested strategies

Moving from 'talking a good game' to successful evidence-informed practice

Rhetoric about being research-/evidence-informed must match reality. The DfE (2017) identified schools where headteachers 'talked a good game' about evidence-informed teaching in their schools, but the reality was that research and evidence were not embedded in day-to-day school practice. So, what do we know that works?

- School leaders are seen to value research. They encourage staff decision-making to start by asking: 'What does the evidence show?'
- School leaders 'nourish' a research culture that encourages knowledge creation. They avoid research becoming 'another thing' added to workload, and they find something else to remove.
- Honest conversations are held about teachers' research literacy and their ability to make research-informed changes to their practice. A research 'readiness audit' is completed to capture an accurate assessment of the level of skills, knowledge and understanding within the school community (see example in Jones 2018: 236).
- Staff have a shared understanding that research is a process of collecting evidence from multiple sources to make informed decisions. 'Academic' research does not replace professional experience. Combining evidence from academic research with school data, practitioner expertise and stakeholder views increases robust decision-making.
- 'Research Champions' or research teams are developed to support the school community and cascade evidence-informed school practices. These staff are research literate, they understand ethical research issues and they have good pedagogical knowledge and excellent people skills.
- Meaningful engagement of school leaders with people who have different views from themselves is seen as a strength, encouraging information and decision-making to be scrutinised.
- Learning conversations where staff and students feel their informed views are listened to are embedded into school practice – avoiding 'pseudo-inquiry' which looks like inquiry but is not driven by a genuine desire to learn.
- 'Cherry-picking' research that doesn't tell the whole story and/or supports a particular message that an individual wants to push is avoided. Transparency is assured.

- Staff are encouraged to come forward with 'bad news' about projects and are asked for suggestions about what can be done to resolve problems.
- Governors/Trustees take account of multiple sources of evidence in their decision-making processes.

Headteachers' views

I regularly survey teachers and their headteachers about taking part in school-based research. Their comments below capture some of the benefits they identified and a teacher's previous misconceptions:

> I thought that research was mostly conducted by 'experts' – those *not* working in schools. Now I know it is a way of getting clear insight into how something is working, and we should not assume we always know what is best for pupils. (Teacher)

> It brought a huge benefit to the quality of teaching and learning in the school. Each educational environment is different, and undertaking action research with *our* boys in the context of national/international research has informed changes in school T&L policy. (Headteacher)

> Having time to focus on one area provides valuable insight into something that can often be overlooked. Progress in writing with targeted children improved; staff are more enthusiastic and engaged. (Headteacher)

> It is a valuable process. It keeps teachers actively involved in the ever-changing education system and helps the whole school. (Headteacher)

> The impact has been a more informed staff who are comfortable using research-based evidence to qualify their opinions. (Headteacher)

Gill Richards

This book

This book describes the work of ten school leaders who initiated new developments in their schools and carried out research studies to measure the impact of these. They aim to share what they learned and, by explaining the processes they used, to help readers understand how these can be replicated.

Case-study research benefits from including the views of everyone involved, especially the views of children, who are typical recipients of education research findings. All the school leaders writing in this book ensured that the perspectives of those involved were ethically included.

The first chapter explores the experiences and learning of new school leaders during their first 100 days in post. The rest of the chapters follow a format that starts with explaining the context and why a specific innovation was selected. This is followed by details of the innovation and how evidence of impact was collected. Each chapter concludes with a discussion of what leaders found and recommendations for practice.

The chapters

In Chapter One, David S Stewart shares the experiences of new headteachers in their first 100 days in post. Key themes are explored, like overcoming challenges in developing new relationships and carrying out change. Successful strategies are described, using practical examples like where one new head urged others to make use of every opportunity that presents itself; after needing a beekeeper to remove a swarm of bees from the playground, she invited him back later to teach the children about bees. The chapter concludes with advice from the new headteachers about the management strategies, support and resources they found particularly helpful.

In Chapter Two, David Anderson explores how it feels to go to the least-desirable school in a catchment area. He reports on the views of Year 9 students who attended a non-selective school located in a community where the other schools are selective. Their experiences highlighted issues of the 11+ selective system, an overarching theme of resilience, and an ultimately positive sense of new beginnings and fresh opportunities. The chapter concludes with recommendations on how school leaders in similar situations could support their students and communicate positive experiences within the wider community to help overcome negative perceptions of attending a non-selective school.

In Chapter Three, James Brown reports on a study that aimed to identify causes of occupational stress experienced by headteachers. It explores whether gender, age, experience level or school Ofsted rating had any significant impact on their experiences. The most common causes of these headteachers' stress were identified as issues of school performance, curriculum, standards, scrutiny and accountability, and the peak times when these occurred were May, June, July and December. The chapter concludes with recommendations for school leaders that can help them plan and seek support to manage the professional challenges that most leaders face on a regular basis.

In Chapter Four, James Hutchinson describes a new approach to appraisal and quality assurance that uses a holistic view of teachers' impact on the children in their classes. He explains how data, evidence of the environment, video clips, photographs, monitored work, pupil voice and more are drawn together, providing easily accessible feedback evidence that enables teachers to reflect on and also learn from colleagues across the school. The chapter details how the system was set up, how it changed over time and how it could be adapted to meet the constantly changing educational environment. The final section includes practical examples of what worked well, its impact and the views of staff about the system. The chapter concludes with recommendations on how this style of appraisal can be developed in different school contexts.

In Chapter Five, Michael Gorton reports on how a research project on lessening teachers' marking workload was led successfully across the whole school. He describes the process of designing and running a project that involved every teacher in the school, covering how momentum was maintained, how evidence was gathered and how the findings were turned into a new school policy. The final section includes the results of leading this research project across the school, providing practical examples of what worked well and how any challenges were overcome. The chapter concludes with recommendations on how to successfully develop a whole-school research project.

In Chapter Six, Chris Wardle reports on how 'Poverty Proofing' – a programme developed by Children North East – was used as a strategy to break the cycle of disadvantage for young people in his school. He describes the methods used by the school to gain an accurate picture of poverty from their students' 'voice' and the processes that followed to translate what was discovered to ensure that school policies and procedures were not disadvantaging pupils. The final section describes the impact these changes made to school practices and concludes with recommendations on how leaders can 'poverty proof' their own schools to maximise students' participation in school life.

In Chapter Seven, Matthew Sammy explores what schools can learn from students' experiences of internal and fixed-term exclusion. He focuses on the experiences of two brothers, their mother and the senior leader who had responsibility for behaviour at the school where the boys attended. It describes the realities of exclusion for these boys and their family and identifies the key themes that arose: effectiveness of exclusion; power; school ethos and policy; SEND needs. The chapter concludes with recommendations for ways in which school leaders can utilise insight into young people's experiences to inform effective school-behaviour policy sanctions.

In Chapter Eight, Leanne Mitchell reports on a school volunteer trip to Ghana to help build an orphanage, reflecting on who benefits. She describes how students were prepared before the trip and the activities involved during the ten-day stay. She then explores the impact on students' experiences and learning, identifying themes from their reflections – like an impact on the way they lived their lives in relation to social media, relationships with family and friends, and helping others. The chapter concludes by considering some of the moral/ethical issues around schools' engagement with charity work and recommends ways in which school leaders can approach charitable volunteering in an empowering way for all involved.

In Chapter Nine, Laura Wookey reports on how she worked with her multi-academy trust (MAT) to co-construct a new curriculum across the Trust. This was underpinned by a determination to offer children a curriculum that would promote compassion, integrity and a pursuit of excellence in order for them to reach their potential and become well-rounded individuals, prepared for the next stage of their education and wider life journey. She describes how the process was rolled out, giving practical examples of what worked well and evidence of impact. She concludes with recommendations on how others could implement a 'lived curriculum' using similar approaches within their own settings.

In Chapter Ten, Emily Walker describes how a group of schools co-operated to carry out Special Educational Needs and Disability (SEND) Reviews by working in triads to investigate the quality of their practice. She explains how the process was carried out and the research methods used to collect evidence of the schools' SEND practice. The final section includes examples of the impact of the review on practice, what worked well in carrying it out and the views of staff who took part. It concludes with recommendations on ways in which school leaders can effectively conduct their own review of SEND provision.

Recommended reading

Jones, G. (2018) *Evidence-Based School Leadership and Management: A Practical Guide*, London: Sage Publications Ltd

References

DfE (2017) *Evidence-Informed Teaching: An Evaluation of Progress in England*. Available online at: www.gov.uk/government/publications (Accessed 11/02/21)

Hattie, J. (2016) *Visible Learning into Action*, Abingdon: Routledge

Jones, G. (2018) *Evidence-Based School Leadership and Management: A Practical Guide*, London: Sage Publications Ltd

Nelson, J., and O'Beirne, C. (2014) *Using Evidence in the Classroom: What Works and Why?* Slough: NfER

Chapter 1

"An overwhelming, scrutinised, roller coaster experience – I love it!"

New headteachers' first 100 days

David S Stewart

Context

"I have great pleasure in offering you the post of headteacher. . . ." Spoken by many a Chair of Governors, thus begins the journey for what must be one of the most responsible positions in any community. Statistics would indicate that this is by no means a popular job, and many communities struggle to appoint. The School Teachers' Review body in its 30th report noted that there is a growing challenge in retaining experienced classroom teachers and those in leadership roles, creating an 'unfolding crisis in leadership supply' (2020: 12). For those who do accept the challenge, what are their expectations, their hopes and aspirations? And what indeed is the reality?

After nearly 40 years in school leadership, 27 as headteacher, one might imagine that it is easy to forget the early days of headship. Not at all. Those first days and weeks are very firmly engrained. A sense of feeling overwhelmed, isolated and out of my depth. What have I taken on? There was the additional pressure of internal promotion. "Is he up to the new role?" I was fortunate to have a supportive governing body, a hard-working staff and very good support and mentoring from the local authority.

Asking five newly appointed headteachers to record their first 100 days in post gave an insight to their individual journeys with the highs and lows. They were asked to detail their particular feelings and experiences at different stages in those 100 days. For teachers seeking to follow in their footsteps, there is much to reflect on. The variety of their starting points was interesting. One experienced head had a year to set up a new school. Another came through promotion within an Academy Trust. Their schools included a small

DOI: 10.4324/9781003104698-2

rural primary school and a hospital school – each with their unique challenges. One required very immediate changes.

The first 100 days

"I was excited about making a real difference."

Having secured their new post, the headteachers recalled a mixture of emotions: "I had no fears of any sort, which is unusual for me. I felt excited with the prospect of the challenge ahead." There was also a sense of shock. "I spent the following three hours after 'the call' saying 'Oh my life I can't believe it.'" Generally, they could not wait to get started. Even the experienced head, whilst being quietly confident, still had the sense of excitement for a new challenge with different pupils and staff.

Before taking on the role of headteacher, previous years of training and experience clearly played an important part. One, who had been a deputy, spoke highly of a head who had "allowed me to shadow every part of the job. The head ensured that I had a clear understanding of the role and accountability that sits with the headteacher." Another agreed that the mentoring they had received whilst a deputy had been invaluable in understanding "budget, finances and HR."

Not all were so fortunate, stating: "I didn't have any mentoring in terms of preparation for leadership and the budget/finances" and "I was never really involved in the HR."

It was evident that the new heads felt that training in HR and budgets was essential, as one explained: "With budgets getting ever more challenging, it is important to have a clear understanding on how you can save money and make money." A real problem for any deputy is a head who is not prepared to share, to offer that apprenticeship model. Learning from this, one new head was already giving their senior leadership opportunity to experience this responsibility: "The knowledge empowers them to make decisions," while another had decided: "Once I appoint a deputy I will mentor in budgets and finance."

Berry (2016) makes much of a good handover from the outgoing head, but there seemed to be little evidence of this amongst the respondents. Clearly circumstances do not always allow this, so it means a great deal of catch up. Neither did the new heads make particular mention of support from a deputy. This was interesting.

One had no deputy, and others referred to the leadership team, but where was the relationship with a deputy? The head who spent 100 days without a SLT was reliant on coaching sessions provided by the Trust, which enabled focus and reflection. And of course, the SLT may include unsuccessful headship candidates. It would be naïve to assume that everyone has got the new head's 'back.'

The euphoria of being offered the post can somewhat diminish as the new term approaches. Self-doubt and unhelpful negative predictions crept in for some:

> I questioned if I had done the right thing. I still felt emotional about leaving my other school.

> Could I do this role to the best of my ability and be accepted by the staff, parents and children?

For a headteacher there are different stakeholders who need to be satisfied: "I had a roller coaster of emotions. I didn't want to let anyone down." Taking over from a long-established head was another anxiety: "Would staff be on board with a new direction in leadership?"

Make sure you prepare for Day 1

"I was really excited and really nervous!"

Preparing for the first day of school was a clear priority and something which needed to be rehearsed: "I wanted staff to have confidence in me, which meant I had to ensure I was confident and strong on the outside." For one head, assuming headship in the time of COVID-19 added to the pressures, as the first contact with staff would be via remote means. Emails were a cause of anxiety, taking longer to write, "so they would be interpreted correctly." How easy it is for things to be misinterpreted by those who might not want change!

The head of the new school had almost a year between the interview and taking up the post, "so a range of emotions had been experienced up to this point." There was a need to remain optimistic but realistic at the same time. Knowing that it had been able to establish an "outstanding team of staff" added to the confidence. The staff all held the same values and vision for the school, and this undoubtedly helped with any self-doubt.

With this range of emotions, each new head approached the day before the start of term in different ways. Some used the day to relax:

> A lot of preparation had already been done so [I] spent the day with my family and walked the dogs along the river. I needed family time to ground me.

Another took on a task which didn't need much thought, such as painting the garden fence! Others, however, felt the need to be immersed in the school:

> I spent the day in school. I wanted to ensure everything was as prepared as it could be, no stone left unturned. Mental preparation also helped. I started to visualise how the first day would go . . . what would I say to staff during the first briefing, etc.

Working on advice they had received whilst a deputy, one head noted, "I wrote out a to-do list. I re-read effective leadership articles that I had used on my NPQH and wrote the first page of my Leadership Log." With so much anticipation it was perhaps not surprising to learn from one head, "I didn't sleep very well as I was worried that I would miss my alarm."

Anxious predictions are unhelpful; we all make them; but predicting that things will go wrong generally leads to anxiety. In reality, actual events never seem as bad. Reflecting at the end of the first day, all respondents felt "an overwhelming feeling of relief that the first day was over." Not only relief, but also a sense of achievement: "As I walked out, I thought, 'I did it!'" In one school, where clearly the school needed to change, there was the sense of being weighed up by the school community:

> They didn't speak to me on my morning and afternoon walk around the playground – they just stared at me! Staff were wary.

When a school has been in special measures or performing under par, there can be a mixture of feelings, dejection, suspicion, anger and a lack of self-worth. For the incoming head, the responsibility to inspire and support whilst giving challenge can be daunting:

> I knew a lot needed doing, I had an overwhelming sense of responsibility. Raise aspirations for all, make them feel loved and worth it.

One head spoke of the realisation of the need "to change the environment from everything being dark to injecting colour. If we all feel loved and valued, then we all move mountains for each other."

Deliver your vision stage-by-stage

"You can't build Rome in a day."

The first week of headship, reality dawns. There has been much debate about the changing role of headship. Woods and Roberts (2019) talk about distributed leadership, where there is an explicit value base for leadership to be exercised collaboratively, and there is certainly much to commend this. The heads mentioned how important their colleagues are, but there will still be times when the buck stops with the individual. Pay differentials suggest that ultimately one person will be held responsible, and a successful team still comes down to the support and guidance of the head. Interestingly, when things go well credit is given to the strength of the team; yet when things go badly wrong, blame is generally laid at the door of the headteacher.

As a new head there can be a real temptation to get involved with everything, but there was a realisation of the need to "sit on my hands and see how those who are leading areas in the school tick or empower the staff in school." A school has many component parts, and one head commented: "I kept finding another layer and another, like peeling an onion!" Some situations cannot wait and need urgent attention, benefiting from a fresh pair of eyes, as one head described:

> Key pupils need a different approach; systems were not working. A structured nurture group will run from next week.

Knowing when to take urgent action is key if education and welfare are at risk. Not everything can be afforded the luxury of a longer overview. One of the standards which marks out a headteacher is to 'identify and analyse complex or persistent problems and barriers and have strategies for improvement' (Department for Education 2020, Standard 8), so meeting every member of staff can be time consuming but extremely beneficial, as one head described:

> I spent quality time engaging them throughout the first week. These conversations helped me to find out who they were and what motivated them.

Being visible to pupils, staff and families is critical. A school will have a reputation locally (even nationally in the case of well-known schools) for good or ill, so a new head will have to work with this, like one explained: "I hosted meet the headteacher coffee mornings and introduced weekly newsletters to increase communication with parents." Being visible, praising the children for their conduct around school whilst developing a culture of high expectation was much appreciated. Beginning headship during the COVID-19 pandemic meant one head had to guide staff through the process of online team meetings, which some found challenging.

Teaching, whilst an exciting and enjoyable profession, can be stressful and taxing at times, and staff need to know that they are valued. Heads were impressed: "Staff work incredibly hard. They are dedicated and resourceful." Thanking them personally for their hard work as they left the building suggested that one new head would be there to support them.

There was even time in the first week to open up the laptop, answer emails and produce policies. One even recruited new staff. For those working in rural areas with poor Wi-Fi coverage, issues of connection added to the pressures.

Stay positive: energy, enthusiasm, hope

> *"Acknowledge mistakes, forgive yourself. Don't be afraid to change direction and move on with humility."*

'It's essential to have energy, enthusiasm and hope' – Brighouse (2007: 8). In defining the character of headship, the author uses *hope* not *optimism*, because there is the promise of delivery: a matter of determination, not opinion. Clearly the new heads were moving forward with great amount of energy and enthusiasm and buckets full of hope!

Having survived the first week, the new heads felt confident to instigate review and make changes. For one, an immediate review of the whole school by the Trust was key in identifying which areas were successful and which areas needed development. External review is always healthy for any school. Better that things are picked up before the Office for Standards in Education, Children's Services and Skills (Ofsted) arrives! Perhaps unsurprisingly, the issue of middle leadership was an early priority with "correct CPD being mapped out." Understanding the role of middle leaders, those who balance a teaching role with wider responsibilities, is important. A report by NAHT (2019) noted that one in three 'middle leaders' were considering leaving the profession, citing a reduction of time and training to carry out the role.

For those whose 100 days included the COVID-19 pandemic there was a steep learning curve, with closures and re-openings which resulted from following the plethora of ever-changing guidelines – hard enough for a seasoned head, but enormously challenging for a new one. There was no-one who could say, "This is how we did it the last time." Support from Trusts appeared to have been very helpful, but on the ground, it was still down to the individual: "Even now [that] we are open I have to adapt and change accordingly." Managing a whole-school change project via the Internet for one head was particularly difficult. Staff felt uneasy, and it took time to reassure them.

There were many other issues to deal with, such as improving the mindset of parents who had previously not felt listened to: "I held an open coffee morning and evening linked to a parents' evening to gauge their feelings to inform my action plan." Even then, not all parents were satisfied, and one head had to deal with complaints from a parent. However professional a headteacher is, it is very hard not to take it personally. Fortunately, in this case it was worked through to a satisfactory conclusion, but it can be a real knock in those early days when a new headteacher is working so hard to do everything right.

Taking on a school where staff had been directionless needed urgent attention because "they were doing their own thing." Being a head is not about being popular, and there will always be difficult situations. The vision for the very best educational experiences for the pupils must always be paramount. Continuing to have one-to-one meetings with staff was certainly of benefit: "I learnt so much by listening and observing staff share their thoughts and beliefs." Staff appraisal enabled heads to set and reinforce their expectations so that staff knew how their role contributed to the school's vision.

Be a brilliant communicator

> "How information is communicated is key."

There is a fine balance to be made in supporting strategic thinking but also allowing staff to own their subject or area of responsibility.

Striking a balance was "key to empowering staff in the school." Admitting that one does not always have the answer gives breathing space. A headteacher needs to be confident to say, "I will get back to you" or to suggest that the person might be able to resolve the situation themselves.

A headteacher can end up with many 'issues' on his or her shoulders, left there by others to resolve. The art of leadership is not to accept them all and to return them to the owner. Not to do so means the head will very quickly be worn down. Whilst encouraging colleagues to manage their personal well-being, one head reminded them not to forget their own 'work/life balance' – "I need to practise what I preach!"

For the head of a new school, the whole staff approach to developing the curriculum was key, notably making reference to "as a staff we" and very clearly recognising themselves as part of the way forward, using many references to *we* rather than *I*. For another there was an innovative project to involve pupils as leaders, grouped in teams to focus on particular priorities within the school's improvement plan: "Children felt empowered to lead their school." As the term progressed, this project went from strength to strength, and the staff team realised that they were "supporting the next generation of leaders."

Make sure you reach out to others

"Ensure you have a strong network of support."

Only one head referred to the governing body as a whole, and this was in terms of giving weekly updates rather than any support coming from governors. Another mentioned a particularly supportive governor. This general lack of acknowledgement is disappointing, for they should be a source of support to a new head. And indeed, governing bodies have a responsibility for holding headteachers to account as well as their appraisal (Barton 2020). If there appears to be little connection with governors, how will they hold the leadership team to account (NGA 2020) for educational performance and quality of teaching and learning?

At the very least, a weekly phone call from the Chair would have been welcome, for headship can be a very lonely role. This is quite apart from the importance that Ofsted places on governance in its reporting: a head needs to ensure that governors fully buy into the vision and support the school's strategic direction, especially when the new head's vision is different from a predecessor's. One head referred to managing this loneliness:

> The feeling of loneliness is strong at times, and I have made sure I reach out to others.

The 'others' might be heads in other authorities or colleagues in former schools. Moving to a new authority can be daunting, as one head found: "Not knowing names of key people to go to is at times unnerving." There were some key colleagues who 'made' the first week for another:

> Every day I have had text or phone call from the Director of Quality Assurance. This has been invaluable in sharing good things, discussing challenges.

Having support as a new head is important, as is being able to recognise one's own limitations and being prepared to seek advice. The new heads identified that mentoring would be invaluable, as would be "to be paired with an experienced head in your first year with all the new things you are learning for the first time."

Be relentless, be resilient, persevere

By the end of the first half-term, whilst there were still feelings of doubt, there was huge amount of optimism. There had been surprising opportunities (such as dealing with a swarm of bees, which was a real nuisance but led to the local beekeeper spending a day in school with the pupils). Heads commented that: "I am absolutely loving my new role, and each day I feel more confident" and "I am stronger than I thought I was." Strategies for bringing staff on board had been developed, as one described: "I am able to use humour to defuse tricky situations."

Even for the more experienced, there had been much to learn. In regard to safeguarding and health and safety, one head reported that: "You know a little, but as a head you need to have a clear overview – ultimately you are responsible for both." There is a wide learning curve, and it was recognised as important to accept this, with one head explaining: "Realising I can't do everything, and I won't know everything, I am still learning." So as half-term approached, the new heads were clearly proud of what they had achieved thus far. Every day is a new day, and as one joked: "Wine helps too!"

Transforming practice

NPQH and CPD

Since 2012, the NPQH is no longer compulsory for headteachers, but most of those who had undertaken it had certainly found it extremely useful:

> I would advise any prospective headteacher to access this qualification prior to starting their first headship.

The leadership elements and self-reflection were found to be particularly useful in supporting a new head and the SLT during challenging times. Apart from the knowledge and skills learnt being on the course, one head explained that:

> It built up a network of support which ensures that I continue to be a self-reflective and an 'ever learning' headteacher.

In terms of CPD, it was felt that the programmes could be part of the performance management/appraisal process of a deputy. One respondent felt that these needed to be adapted for those coming from different sectors of the education system, in particular, on the thorny issue of support staff.

As weeks went on, the heads now felt confident to take the schools forward. Looking back on their first 100 days, there still appeared to be a love of the job, a feeling of passion, a sense of pride: "I still feel excited about the journey I am on with my school." There had been undoubted challenges and moments of frustration, but there were still comments such as: "The majority of time I really do love this new role."

Central to the ethos of all the schools was the learning of pupils, and so creating an environment in which both pupils and staff could flourish was critical:

> We created a culture of wanting to try new pedagogy; staff would go and watch each other and share their practice.

All the new heads knew that there was still much to do. Support from others had also been critical: "The Trust enabled me to stay focussed on continuing to be strategic."

And what advice would these new headteachers give to others?

1. Start to create the culture you wish to see from the minute you walk through the door.
2. To be paired with an experienced head would be invaluable, especially in your first year.
3. Empower your SLT internally in school, and have a network out of school to support you.
4. Listen to the opinions of others, and be confident in the vision of the school.
5. Be assertive when required.
6. Have the balance of being open to change, but equally believe and be confident in the school's ethos and aims.
7. There will be problems; there will be setbacks. You will deal with them, and you will overcome them. Be kind to yourself.

References

Barton, M. (2020) *Headteacher Appraisal: A Guide for Governing Boards*, Birmingham: NGA

Berry, J. (2016) *Making the Leap – Moving from Deputy to Head*, Carmarthen: Crown Publishing Ltd

Brighouse, T. (2007) *How Successful Head Teachers Survive and Thrive*, Birmingham: RM Publishers

Department for Education (2020) *Headteachers' Standards 2020*, London: Department for Education

NAHT (2019) *About Time: Life as a Middle Leader*, Haywards Heath: NAHT

National Governance Association (NGA) (2020) *A View from the Board: Ofsted's New Education Inspection Framework*, Birmingham: NGA

School Teachers' Review Body (2020) *30th Report*, London: Office of Manpower Economics

Woods, P., and Roberts, A. (2019) Collaborative School Leadership in a Global Society: A Critical Perspective, *Educational Management Administration & Leadership*, 47(5): 663–677

Chapter 2

Bottom of the pile?

How does it feel to go to the least desirable school in the area?

David Anderson

Context

I recently took a taxi ride from a station to attend a meeting. During the 10-minute journey, I talked with the driver about the schools in the area. "I wouldn't want my grandchildren to go to that school," she said, referring to my destination. She then proceeded to describe the hierarchy of local schools, with an independent school at the top, a grammar school, then a faith school, followed by a series of less- and less-desirable comprehensive academies. The pattern would be similar in any town or city in England, and it demonstrates the stratified and segregated education system we have.

I have always been passionate about working in schools that truly serve their local communities – *all* the children in their communities, regardless of background, faith or ability. I was keen to find out what it feels like to go to a school that is the least desirable in an area – what we might call 'the bottom of the pile.' Would those students be demoralised by their experiences of apparent failure in a system designed to separate the winners from the losers? Or would they feel more comfortable working alongside students with similar experiences? And what about their futures – was there optimism for opportunities and growth or a sense of resignation? I felt that the voices of students in non-selective schools in areas where some schools select by ability (grammar schools) were absent from the educational narrative, and I wanted to capture young peoples' experiences of the 11-plus (the test that decides whether they can attend a selective school), their attitudes towards school

DOI: 10.4324/9781003104698-3

now and some of their aspirations for the remainder of their schooling. I also wanted to share these insights with school leaders, so that this could help them shape the way they interact with students and parents, and perhaps raise the status of their school in the community.

Midtowne schools

The study was carried out in a town (Midtowne) in the Midlands where there are five state secondary schools within the town itself, plus one in a rural location. Two of the schools in the town are single-sex selective grammar schools. The other four are non-selective schools with differing intake, educational outcomes and reputation. Table 2.1 outlines the principal characteristics of the six schools in Midtowne. (All names have been changed.)

A few observations are noteworthy from this table. The two single-gender selective schools are both rated 'Outstanding' by Ofsted, but they also have a low proportion of students on free school meals and with English as an additional language in comparison to the other schools. There is also an apparent trend between Progress 8 figures and the percentage of students on free school meals – as the percentage of FSM increases, the Progress 8 figures decrease.

East Bridge Academy is the focus of this study. It is characterised by having 407 students on roll (it is currently undersubscribed), with the lowest academic outcomes in the area and a high proportion of disadvantaged students, including those for whom English is an additional language. Ofsted (the government's school inspection service) rated the school as 'Inadequate' (the lowest of 4 ratings) in its most recent inspection to our study. Within the student population, there are a range of attitudes and experiences concerning the 11-plus test, for example students who had taken the 11-plus and not passed and students who had not taken the test.

The students involved in the research study were in Year 9 (ages 13–14) and took part in focus groups where they were prompted to describe their thoughts, feelings and emotions as they progressed through Year 6 (ages 10–11) into secondary school transition and then on to Year 9.

Table 2.1 School characteristics

Secondary league Table position according to schoolguide.co.uk	School	Gender	Intake	Status	Age range	Number on roll	Ofsted rating	% FSM	% EAL	Progress 8 2017	Attainment 8 2017	% 9–4 (A*-C) 2017
1	Midtowne Grammar	Boys	Selective	Academy	11–18	1119	Outstanding	2.6	5	0.41	66.3	100
2	The Queen Anne School	Girls	Selective	Academy	11–18	1199	Outstanding	2.6	3	0.65	68.1	98
3	Ridge End Academy	Girls (mixed 6th)	Comprehensive	Academy	11–18	733	Good	9.6	7	0.37	48.6	74
4	Trinity Meadows Academy	Mixed	Comprehensive	Academy	11–18	1238	Outstanding	9.9	11	0.52	44.9	56
Not rated	The Horizon School	Mixed	Comprehensive	Academy	11–16	215	Good	25.6	3	0.09	42.3	52
Not rated	East Bridge Academy	Mixed	Comprehensive/ Church of England	Academy	11–16	407	Inadequate	22.4	12	−0.91	29.6	28

Transforming practice

The aim of my research was to help school leaders working in selective areas to have a better understanding of how students think and feel about their journey from Year 6 to Year 9 through some firsthand accounts – what are the perceptions of students who do not go to a selective school, how do they view the process of selection and what impact has it had on them? As Reay (2017: 69) says:

> There is no getting away from the emotional repercussions of being positioned at the bottom of the educational market, in the lower reaches of the Local Authority league tables.

Similarly, Coe *et al.* (2008) highlight the argument that is often put forward against selective schools, whereby students who do not pass the 11-plus experience damaging feelings of rejection and failure: 'Rejected pupils may see themselves as failures and intrinsically worth less than those who succeed' (page 22).

Through my research I was keen to find answers to these three questions:

1. What do students think about selection, and what impact has it had on them?
2. What are the 'emotional repercussions' of attending the least favourable school in the area?
3. Do students attending non-selective schools actually exhibit greater resilience and strength as a result of their 'failure' in the 11-plus, or do they see themselves as academic failures with low self-esteem?

Collecting evidence to measure impact

Evidence collection

I arranged to visit the school to collect evidence from two focus groups (one was all female and the other, all male) which the deputy head organised. Each group consisted of five students, and the protocol was identical for each group. I chose focus groups because they:

- Are more time-efficient than individual interviews
- Allow for cross-checking of views and different perspectives to be shared

- Are recommended for finding out the views of marginalised or under-represented groups.

I followed research literature advice for conducting the focus groups (Sinner *et al.* 2018). For example, it suggested that single-gender groups of unfamiliar students with an age range of less than two years are most suitable, so I chose Year 9 students since they had some perspective to look back upon the events from Year 6 onwards coupled with the emotional maturity to understand the lines of inquiry. The Year 9 students were also the new headteacher's first cohort since joining the school.

Recruitment of suitable student participants was recognized as a challenge and discussed with the deputy. We were aware of issues of bias, for example:

- Range of student background and circumstances – with a small sample, it would be hard to capture the full range.
- Student willingness to participate – those students most likely to accept being involved may not have representative views.
- Selection of potential students by the deputy head – the perceived view of the 'best' students for the focus groups may not be representative. (Whilst there was an attempt to choose a cross-section of students, there is always inherent bias in selecting such a small sample of students.)

The room was laid out conference-style, with seats around the table for the five participants, me and the deputy head. The deputy head's role was to provide a familiar and reassuring presence throughout the session in case the discussion unlocked emotions or raised questions that the students had not yet confronted, to provide me with additional context to some of the students' responses and to give support if necessary. Of course, the presence of a senior teacher in the focus group may have affected the nature of the responses of the students. We tried to mitigate against this by using ice-breaker questions at the start and by trying to create a relaxed atmosphere.

There were 17 questions in total, and both focus group sessions lasted around 45 minutes. Audio recordings of the sessions were made on a tablet, then transcribed and coded, as described later. The sequence of events (described in the following text) was kept the same for each focus group.

Icebreaker

The first part of the session began with icebreaker questions such as: "If you could pick a super-power, what would it be?" This was to engage the students, to help make them feel at ease and to encourage them to start to talk openly about their views and experiences.

The Journey map

The students were then talked through 'The Journey map' (Figure 2.1) – an A3 visual prompt handed out.

The aim of this 'map' was to help the students visualise the journey they had been on from Year 6 – through the time of the 11-plus, receiving their secondary-school offer, starting at secondary school and up to their current time in Year 9 and beyond. It was hoped that this visual prompt would help students remember more accurately their feelings, thoughts and actions at different times in the past.

After describing the journey map, the main questions were posed, using the map to show which stage in their education the questions related to. For example:

- A little later in the year some of you and your friends had their 11-plus results. How was it at that time? Can you remember how you felt?
- Then in March, you found out which school you were being offered. Did you get your first choice? How did you feel when you found out you had been offered a place at East Bridge Academy?
- Were any of your friends offered different schools from you? How did that make you feel?
- What was the reputation of East Bridge Academy in the community like before you joined the school?
- When you first started at East Bridge Academy, how was it different from what you had expected?
- Now you are in Year 9. When you look back at Year 6, how do you feel about the 11-plus?
- Now that you have been at East Bridge for nearly three years, how has your opinion of the school changed?

The intention was to try and ask each question and then to hold back as far as possible and allow the students to feed off one

28 David Anderson

"The Journey" –
Prompt to aid focus
group discussions

Figure 2.1 The Journey map

another's responses and to talk naturally. They were encouraged to talk to each other and to share their thoughts and feelings. I was conscious that the actions of myself and the deputy could influence their contributions – for example, we might give non-verbal encouragement or suggest empathy through nodding or facial expressions or by verbal acknowledgements, so we tried to avoid doing this to remain as neutral as possible.

After the focus group sessions, the audio recordings were transcribed. The transcripts were analysed using a coding system. Fourteen codes were identified in total (Table 2.2), and these were analysed further to identify themes that are discussed in the 'Impact' section.

Ethics

The research was conducted in keeping with the BERA ethical guidelines (2018). All the questions to be asked during the focus groups were checked by the deputy head and the school's headteacher, who also suggested some extra questions to further their own understanding of student perceptions. All the student participants had written parental consent, and they were given the opportunity to opt out of the research after the introduction stage.

Table 2.2 Codes

C1	Regret not doing 11-plus
C2	Regret not working hard enough to pass
C3	Self-affirming strategies to cope with disappointment
C4	Coping strategies
C5	Damaged relationships
C6	Fresh start
C7	Lack of academic worth
C8	Building new academic capital
C9	Background leading to low aspirations
C10	Emotional effect of 11-plus
C11	Reputation of school affected by 11-plus
C12	Lack of academic aspiration – link to background?
C13	Thoughts on taking the 11-plus test
C14	Parental perspective effect on student perspective

The deputy and I discussed the importance of students not feeling obliged to take part, since it would be hard for a student to say 'no' to such a request from a senior teacher. The issue of 'avoidance of harm' was considered important. It was imperative that the students were offered the opportunity to explore any questions or unlocked emotions brought about by the study, so the deputy head made time available to them in the days that followed.

The names of all participants, schools and locations have been changed to preserve anonymity, and everyone was advised of this prior to taking part in the research. The host school received anonymised summary data from the questions, in addition to a full paper report.

Impact

The overarching theme that emerged from all the student participants was resilience. Whilst circumstances had led them to attend what one of the students described as a "garbage school," there was a sense of new beginnings and fresh opportunities, and they were ultimately positive about their current position.

Within this main theme, five supplementary themes were identified. The title of each is described by a direct quote from one of the students that summarises that theme.

"So, we kind of huddled together."

Most of the students talked at length about how the 11-plus had affected their relationships with their peers. Here, Ben describes how he and his friends coped with the immediate aftermath of the 11-plus results and secondary school offers:

> A lot of other friends were going to other schools, so we kind of split up and divided our friend group, but I had a bunch of people with me so we kind of huddled together and we stuck it out.

Sam was the only one to overtly report of a broken friendship as a result of the 11-plus. He referred to two of his friends who were planning to go to the same school, but when one of them was offered a place at the grammar school, "their friendship died down.

You would always see them together, but at the end of Year 6 they would just never talk to each other." He also mentioned a pair of friends who had passed the 11-plus and "felt really bad because we were there, and we didn't pass, and they were really happy."

"One mark off"

Izzy, mournful at friendships lost, was even more regretful at not having attended revision sessions for the 11-plus since she was only one mark short of a pass. She was modest in her description of her emotions in relation to this situation:

> I was a bit upset that I didn't get in. I was disappointed, and I was regretting not going to the (revision) sessions, but those who did get in, I did never feel jealous because I knew what they would go on to do and their capabilities, so I just congratulated them.

"Garbage school"

The students expressed a variety of pre-conceived ideas of what the school would be like before they joined. Hollie's response was typical of the others: "I was told it was one of the worst schools in the country." Sam presented the title taken for this theme: "What people were saying was that it is basically a garbage school."

However, the recurrent attitude of the participants to the school's poor reputation tallies with the overarching theme of resilience. In response to the negativity, many of the participants added that they did not believe what they were being told. As Alfie neatly summarises here:

> But I just didn't listen to them. . . . And how could they know if they don't have any siblings who went there, they are just judging them by their surroundings.

Other students talked about how the school was better than they had initially perceived it to be:

> In a way I'm actually kind of glad I didn't pass because at this school I have learnt not even just academic skills, I've learnt

> new different things from the people I have met here that have taught me things that you normally wouldn't just learn by yourself. My opinion has completely changed – I think that this school is really, really good. The teachers do a really good job of helping the students.

Another student added more evidence that the school is having a positive effect:

> I think everything the school is doing is helping immensely. Because, if you think about it, if you help students to get good grades, and the best that they can get, then those students are going to go off and find good jobs and go to College and all that; they are going to have to talk to people about their experiences, and they are going to pass on. We have already seen parts of that already in the community. I prefer it a lot, being around the school because in Year 7 it was pretty scary, but now you know places and it's nicer to see people; everyone's always smiling, so it's helping a lot with the community.

"*The right school for me*"

Throughout the discussions, most of the students made comments that revealed what could be described as defence mechanisms, coping strategies or standpoints to build new academic capital by making a fresh start. For example, when Alfie described his school as the "right school for me," he was putting to one side the emotional after-effects he suffered at taking and not passing the 11-plus. He had constructed a sense that he is now in the best school for him academically. Despite his apparent academic modesty, however, he had aspirations:

> I'm trying to be the first person in my family to go to University, so I've just got to work really hard to get there. I'm quite happy that I didn't pass because if I had passed, I wouldn't have done as well in the lessons that I do here.

"*That's every child's fear – disappointing their parents*"

There were a variety of parental approaches to the 11-plus. For example, two of the students described a forceful approach by their parents, and their language was emotive as illustrated by Sam in this extract:

> My parents wanted me to do it. Mine were very pushy. They made me prepare through the entire year.

Alfie described in detail how his parents had nagged him to revise in the lead up to the 11-plus (including the school holidays), and how much he hated it and found it difficult to do, while at the same time faced with the dilemma of wanting to make his parents proud. Here, he gives an honest insight into his motivation at that time:

> Obviously at that age you want to impress your mum and dad as much as you can.

Other parents' attitudes were shaped by their own experiences of secondary school. One student explained his regret at not being entered for the 11-plus by his parents, as he would like to have known how he would have gotten on. Since his siblings had all gone to East Bridge Academy, he was given no choice by his parents, and I suspect he resented this decision.

Conclusion

My overarching conclusion was that, despite attending the least favourable school in the area, the majority of students were positive about their school. They were resilient to the challenges of the 11-plus test and the subsequent transition to different schools, and for some of them, the failure of the 11-plus test had been a strengthening process. The students appeared to have developed a range of coping strategies and defence mechanisms to help them deal with the emotional repercussions of the 11-plus and had, broadly speaking, built a positive working environment to inhabit in their school. This was something the students had largely built for themselves, although they did make reference to the school providing the help and support they needed.

Recommendations

Recommendations for practice

While the context and circumstances of the East Bridge Academy are unique to the school and the time of my research, there are some general recommendations for school leaders in similar schools that I think can be taken from this research study:

1 Find out what your students really thought about the school before they joined. This will give you a flavour of some of the possible misconceptions that can then be addressed in promotional materials.
2 Find out what students think has helped them most in building their academic self-esteem. Use this as one of your unique selling points.
3 Use student ambassadors to help build and improve the reputation of your school in the community. Increase the use of student voice and alumni in your primary visits and prospective parent videos.

Recommended reading

Crehan, L. (2016) *Cleverlands*, London: Unbound
This very 'readable' book provides insight into how other countries organise their education systems. It highlights the contrasts and similarities with our own system and reminds us that the English education system is not the only, nor the necessarily the best, system.

Sahlberg, P. (2021) *Finnish Lessons 3.0*, London: Teachers College Press
This gives a comprehensive tour through the history and establishment of the much-lauded Finnish education system, which, by stark contrast to the English education system, has equity as its founding principle.

Benn, M. (2018) *Life Lessons*, London: Verso
Benn is a long-time campaigner for comprehensive education, and her book provides an analysis of our current system and a proposal for a National Education Service, much like the NHS – available to all, free at point of service.

Gorard, S. (2018) *Education Policy, Evidence of Equity and Effectiveness*, Bristol: Policy Press
This analyses English educational policy and its effectiveness over the last 20 years, combined with international comparisons and suggestions for the future.

References

British Education Research Association (BERA) (2018) *Ethical Guidelines for Educational Research*, London: BERA

Coe, R., Jones, K., Searle, J., Kokotsaki, D., Kosnin, A.M., and Skinner, P. (2008) *Evidence on the Effects of Selective Educational Systems*, A Report for the Sutton Trust, CEM Centre, Durham University. Available online at: www.gov.gg/CHttpHandler.ashx?id=97485&p=0 (Accessed 10/02/21)

Reay, D. (2017) *Miseducation: Inequality, Education and the Working Classes*, Bristol: Policy Press

Sinner, P., Prochazka, F., Paus-Hasebrink, I., and Farrugia, L. (2018) *What Are Some Good Approaches to Conducting Focus Groups with Children?* Research Toolkit, Department of Media and Communications, London School of Economics and Political Science. Available online at: http://wwww.lse.ac.uk/media-and-communications/assets/documents/research/eu-kids-online/toolkit/frequently-asked-questions/FAQ-34.pdf (Accessed 10/02/21)

Chapter 3

Avoiding headteacher stress

James Brown

Context

I have worked for a Multi-Academy Trust (MAT) in the Midlands since 2013. We are a MAT with a Teaching School Alliance (TSA), School Centred Initial Teacher Training provision (SCITT) and other complementary partnerships which help our pupils succeed. Our schools have a wide-ranging context which presents challenges for the MAT and for the headteachers of each of the schools. I work with headteachers daily and find myself intrigued by the wide-ranging responsibilities they have and the challenges they face as leaders of large groups of staff and pupils. It is this experience that inspired my interest in researching the main causes of headteachers' stress. I wanted to better understand what was causing them the most stress in their roles.

Experiencing stress in the workplace (occupational stress) is normal; indeed stress can be a positive thing, leading to increased arousal, helping us to be prepared and nervous about an event or situation. Conversely, we also know that prolonged periods of exposure to stress can be a negative thing, leading to physiological and psychological harm and ultimately, burn-out. We all perhaps have observed this happening with someone whom we have worked with, or even experienced it ourselves.

The teaching profession is known to be a stressful career choice. Recent studies claim that over 75% of teachers in England reported to have suffered stress because of their jobs, citing anxiety, depression and panic attacks amongst some of the side effects. In other public services such as the police and nursing, stress is also common; but research findings tell us that teachers appear to experience this in greater volumes due to the 'emotional

DOI: 10.4324/9781003104698-4

labour' required to teach and support pupils' development (Hilary et al. 2018).

Teachers also experience excellent levels of reported job satisfaction – mainly due to the feeling of making a difference in children's lives and the relationships formed within the school community. However, whilst there are high levels of job satisfaction, the teaching profession struggles to strike a balance between job satisfaction and stress levels, which has contributed to a teacher recruitment crisis over the past 10 years.

Due to a reduction in available teaching staff and other factors, the role of a headteacher is arguably more stressful than teaching full time. From my professional experience, teaching on the national professional qualifications in school leadership and working closely with aspirant school leaders, there is without doubt concern about the lack of leaders wanting to progress to headship due to the reported pressure and challenges of the role.

So, what other factors might be considered when thinking about the main causes of stress?

Research by Greany and Higham (2018) makes the case that a complex, ever-changing education system and increased parental choice is causing headteachers to feel highly stressed, due to the amount of uncertainty and change headteachers need to cope with.

There have been numerous studies since 1988 which attempt to identify some of the potential causes of stress, however there is a notable lack of recent research which explores this in the current educational and political systems.

Transforming practice

Inspired by my close working relationships with headteachers and some knowledge of their day-to-day stresses, I conducted my research with a view to better understand the specific parts of their jobs that were causing the most stress and share this to improve working conditions for headteachers. Could changing planning and policy help support the role of headteachers to reduce stress and increase job satisfaction? I wanted to see if contextual factors had any influence upon stress levels, so I gathered information about the following variables to help create groupings in my data:

- Time of year
- Experience level

- Gender
- Schools' Ofsted ratings
- Membership of Multi-Academy Trusts (MAT)

I carried out a thematic analysis of related literature, which provided five commonly reported 'stressful areas of work' for headteachers, broadly aligning to their job description (see Table 3.1). I used these themes as a core part of my research design to help frame the question for participants.

Table 3.1 Themes

Theme title	Description and example duties
Change management and policy shift	Creating and maintaining strategic vision
	Gaining staff efficacy
	Responding to government policy
Stakeholder management	Managing expectations and reporting to:
	Parents
	Governors
	Community
	Local Authority
	Multi-Academy Trust
	and/or other body
School business management	Managing school estates
	Budget management
	Risk management
	Legal systems
	Completing general administration
Human resourcing (HR)	Teacher/leader performance
	Quality and quantity of staffing
	Performance management
	Dealing with under-performance, misconduct or conflict
	Recruitment and retention
School performance, curriculum, standards, scrutiny and accountability	Challenges of school context
	Safeguarding
	Pupil outcomes
	External expectations
	Ofsted/HMI
Other	Opportunity for sharing individual causes of workplace stress

Collecting evidence to measure impact

Evidence collection

I created an online questionnaire to collect for my research responses that would be accessible and wide-reaching. I recognised there were some limitations to using a questionnaire for gathering data about people's lived experiences, but I felt this was the best approach to take to ensure I received a sizable response to my survey. I provided open text boxes so respondents could add contextual detail if they wanted to.

The questionnaire collected information in three parts:

- Part 1 – contextual information to help determine any differences in responses from the headteachers
- Part 2 – headteachers' experiences of stress in different months of the year, to identify which were the most stressful times of the year
- Part 3 – headteachers' views on which of the thematic areas of headship were the most stressful on a weekly, termly and annual basis, to help understand how elements of their role changed during the year.

The questionnaire was shared using my existing networks and networks of TSAs, MATs, local authorities and other partners, which resulted in 65 completed responses for analysis.

Impact

The headteacher group

The demographic of those who responded to my survey broadly represented national demographics. Responses showed that:

- 71% were female, and 29% were male
- 63% were in their first headship, and 37% had been a head for less than 3 years (classed as new heads)
- 65% were part of a MAT
- 84% had school Ofsted gradings of 'Good' or higher, and 16% 'Require[d] improvement' or were 'Inadequate'
- On average the headteachers had 357 pupils in their schools.

Time of year – when do headteachers feel the most stressed?

I wanted to get some consensus about when the headteachers experienced the most stress during the year. Responses showed that stress levels are **highest** during May (73%), June (66%), July (53%) and December (51%): headteachers reported the largest frequency of responses in the 'Extremely' or 'Very stressful' categories at these times. Reported stress levels were at their **lowest** during August (78%), September (33%) and February (31%), with headteachers reporting the largest frequency of responses in the 'Mildly' or 'Not at all stressful' categories.

My research did not ask for further information about the causes of stress at these times of year explicitly, but I expect primary headteachers reading this will relate to their links with annual pupil assessments, budget setting, recruitment of teachers and exam seasons. Whilst these research findings might not seem ground-breaking, it may be reassuring to learn that there are times of year that are stressful in general for headteachers.

What causes the most stress for headteachers?

I asked headteachers to report on their stress levels relating to certain themes of work (see Table 3.1) in different timeframes. I wanted to know whether there were roles or pressures that caused stress more or less frequently, or whether some causes were consistent year-round. I asked headteachers to rate their stress levels using a five-point Likert scale from 'Not at all stressful' to 'Extremely stressful' for each theme and across three timeframes. For example:

> *'To what extent do the following activities cause occupational stress on a WEEKLY basis?'*

Table 3.2 shows the weekly and overall annual stress level responses from the headteacher respondents. I have presented the percentage of responses which were in the highest two stress scores as either 'Very' or 'Extremely stressful' to demonstrate what causes stress on a weekly basis and overall, across a year.

Table 3.2 shows clear evidence that the largest and most prominent cause of stress is linked to issues of school performance. In some respects, this finding is reassuring, after all, headteachers are motivated by ensuring that pupils achieve their best possible

Table 3.2 Thematic causes on a weekly basis and annual basis

Stress type	% of headteachers reporting 'Very' or 'Extremely stressful' responses	
	Weekly	Annual
Change management and policy shift	22%	37%
Stakeholder management	43%	40%
School business management	19%	32%
Human resourcing	41%	58%
School performance, curriculum, standards, scrutiny and accountability	52%	80%

outcomes and so will naturally apply pressure upon themselves and their teams to ensure this happens. Headteachers spend large amounts of their time supporting teachers in planning curricula, assessing pupil progress, planning interventions, and working with parents to ensure that their children thrive in school; so this is naturally going to be the root of some level of stress. Several respondents referenced 'External challenge' as being a cause for stress, and many headteachers reading this will know that 'external' pressures from Ofsted, local authorities, MATs and other accountability bodies are likely to be the cause of most stress.

The second-most stressful activity for headteachers was HR, and this was an ongoing pressure that grew across the year. We know that dealing with teacher performance, managing sickness, absence and supply teachers can be hard for leaders to manage. Over the past 10 years we have experienced a shortage in the supply of teachers in the profession for schools to recruit, which respondents also cited as a challenge. There is no doubt that headteachers are spending more time than ever before managing HR in school, hence the rise of school business professionals working in and for schools to support this. In contrast, it was interesting to learn that the lowest responses to stress were linked to school business management. When HR responsibilities are removed, setting and overseeing school budgets, risk management and general administration appear to be less stressful now than they were in the past. How does this compare to your experiences of headship?

There were a number of additional comments made by the headteachers about stress which provide more context to the data collected. Here are a two which you might relate to:

> Human Resources causes stress around recruitment and retention due to finance difficulties. Balancing the need for high quality staff in an RI school and ensuring our budget is balanced is difficult. By taking away resources, the school is less desirable to work in, and therefore retention of staff becomes a more difficult aspect to manage, and stress levels are certainly raised until the May 31st resignation deadline date!

> General health issues – mental and physical for staff, children and parents. Child protection and safeguarding issues. Social well-being issues – i.e. discussing domestic violence, drugs, etc. with parents or children.

Who experiences the most stress?

One of the key questions I wanted to explore was whether the context of a headteacher had any bearing on the level of stress they experience. To demonstrate this, I took all the survey responses using a scalar rating system and created a stress score for each respondent. I then grouped participants to see how these responses differed between groups/contexts. Table 3.3 shows the results:

Table 3.3 Stress levels by groups

Headteacher group	Group average scalar stress score (out of 15)
Ofsted rated 'Inadequate' (1)	7.95
Ofsted rated 'Requires improvement' (9)	7.37
Ofsted rated 'Good' (36)	10.38
Ofsted rated 'Outstanding' (19)	9.62
Non-MAT (23)	10.52
MAT (42)	9.43
Female (46)	9.86
Male (19)	9.77
Experienced (41)	9.8
Inexperienced (24)	9.85
Whole Group Average	**9.46**

This process provided the following findings:

- The *least* stressed group of headteachers are those who are in schools which have been judged by Ofsted as 'Requires improvement' or 'Inadequate,' with stress scores of 7.37 and 7.95 respectively.

  Of the 10 headteachers in those schools, five were experienced (more than three years in headship) and five were classed as inexperienced (less than three years' experience); eight of the schools are part of a MAT. Previous research by Darmody and Smyth (2016) provides evidence that headteachers working in more 'challenging' circumstances do experience higher levels of stress, so I wonder to what extent the school improvement support offered to these schools in recent years has affected the experience and feelings of these headteachers.

- Inexperienced headteachers had an average stress score of 9.8 across the year, broadly in line with the whole-group average score, presenting no case for experience being a factor in increased or decreased stress levels.

- The highest average stress scores came from headteachers whose schools were not part of a MAT and those that Ofsted rated as 'Good' schools, scoring 10.52 and 10.38 respectively. My experience tells me that a key cause for stress in those from 'Good' schools is linked to Ofsted. We know that under the current framework, Ofsted will visit a 'Good' school at least every four years, and the pressure to remain 'Good' is different from that of 'Outstanding' schools, who are currently not being inspected unless there is a safeguarding concern or significant performance issue.

Statistical testing

I also conducted some statistical t-tests to see whether groupings of headteachers had any significantly different experiences. I tested four groups as a part of this analysis.

- Experienced vs inexperienced
- Male vs female
- MAT vs non-MAT
- Ofsted rating of 'Good' or 'Better' vs 'Requires improvement' or lower

Throughout all tested categories, the only significant finding from my analysis was between those in a MAT and those not in a MAT: headteachers in MATs reported lower overall levels of stress compared to that of headteachers who are not in a MAT. This makes me wonder whether the experience of collaboration, shared accountability and shared business functions for those in MATs is leading to an overall sense of protection and reduced stress levels. I also wonder whether those defined as 'Non-MAT' may be experiencing heightened stress levels because they could be isolated and lacking support in an increasingly fragmented education system.

I want to assert that I am not suggesting that a simple way to reduce stress is to join a MAT, as we know that all MATs work differently and so experiences of headteachers will differ – but it is potentially an area for further interesting research. Until this study took place, I found no specific research comparing stress experiences of headteachers in a MAT to those who are not.

Recommendations

Recommendations for practice

Experiencing stress is nothing new, but I have observed that stress levels do appear to have increased over the past ten years, and the causes of stress change as the education sector requires headteachers to adapt to rapidly moving national policy. Not only is policy shift a challenge, but in more recent times the emergence of COVID-19 has completely transformed the role of headteachers, who are temporarily dealing with managing health and safety of school sites on levels never experienced before. In my experience, headteachers are without doubt, courageous, resilient and adaptable public servants; however to support their ongoing development in managing stress, I have identified the following recommendations from this study:

1 Professional networking for headteachers is incredibly important. This study suggested that being involved in a MAT helped reduce headteacher stress levels, and whilst there would need to be additional, extensive research to further evidence this point, networking and sharing of challenges and successes is likely to be vital for headteachers to thrive.

Points to consider: Who is in your support network? What do you gain from this? How do you need to expand this network or make it more useful for you as a headteacher?

2   The pressure of an accountability culture is increasingly stressful and is undoubtably a cause of attrition in the profession. So, it is important that headteachers work together to help prepare and safeguard themselves from 'cliff-edge' inspections. Headteachers should invest time in creating peer review/challenge networks to help keep their practice in school current, to help staff feel more prepared for external scrutiny and to help them have a voice with Ofsted and the DFE in order to create more balance in the accountability system.

    Points to consider: What close peer networks are you a part of, and does this have the rigour you need to help prepare for inspection? Do you have a voice in the system, and how are you using it to effect change?

3   There is very little formal support for headteachers to help them deal with stress, and such support does not form part of any formal teacher and leader professional development. There is an unwritten expectation that headteachers learn how to deal with stress, and I worry that the system needs to be doing more to help prepare aspirant headteachers for the role. I would encourage colleagues to access coaching support and be open with other trusted colleagues about their challenges, while remaining solution-focussed about how best they can help reduce personal stress levels by making change.

    Points to consider: What are you doing to help yourself become more resilient to stress? Who do you turn to? What formal support are you putting in place for yourself to help you thrive?

4   Planning is essential. In general, we know when the most stressful times are during the year. Headteachers should plan for stressful periods of the year, releasing capacity of other leaders or seeking support from external partners during difficult times.

    Points to consider: How does your planning consider stressful periods? Who are you working with to reduce the burden at difficult times of the year?

Recommended reading

These are all selected due to the depth and usefulness of research, despite some being over 10 years old.

Bristow, M., Ireson, G., and Coleman, A. (2007) *A Life in the Day of a Headteacher: A Study of Practice and Well-being*, Nottingham: National College for School Leadership (NCSL)

Darmody, M., and Smyth, E. (2016) Primary School Principals' Job Satisfaction and Occupational Stress, *International Journal of Educational Management*, 30(1): 115–128

Hilary, J., Andrade, J., and Worth, J. (2018) *Teacher Retention and Turnover Research Research Update 4: How Do Teachers Compare to Nurses and Police Officers?* 4th ed., Slough: National Foundation for Education Research (NFER)

Howard, M.L. (2012) *Headteacher Stress, Coping Strategies and Supports: Implications for an Emotional Health*. Available online at: www.research. manchester.ac.uk/portal/en/theses/headteacher-stresscoping-strategies-and-supportsimplications-for-an-emotional-health-and-wellbeing-programme-for-headteachers%28cf0ddf1c-f8cf-410a-b211-2c21bc 59a4bd%29.html (Accessed 09/02/21)

References

Darmody, M., and Smyth, E. (2016) Primary School Principals' Job Satisfaction and Occupational Stress, *International Journal of Educational Management*, 30(1): 115–128

Greany, T., and Higham, R. (2018) *Hierarchy, Markets and Networks*, London: UCL Institute of Education Press

Hilary, J., Andrade, J., and Worth, J. (2018) *Teacher Retention and Turnover Research Research Update 4: How Do Teachers Compare to Nurses and Police Officers?* 4th ed., Slough: National Foundation for Education Research (NFER)

Chapter 4

Appraisal and quality assurance – a deeper deep dive

A holistic approach to changing the culture of performance management

James Hutchinson

Context

My background is in mainstream and special education. I have taught and held senior positions in both sectors, and now as headteacher in a special school I am staggered by how similar the systems are. Learning, children, teaching and teachers are similar in all schools and face the same highs and lows, successes and failures. One thing that remains the same is the process of the observation of teachers to inform appraisal or quality assurance. My issue is that I'm not convinced it tells the whole story.

Early in my teaching career I realised that the most important and *stressful* week, day and lesson of the year was the 'performance management observation.' Although this was over 20 years ago and after moving from head of department to head of faculty, to senior leadership in three different mainstream schools and then on to special education and headship, I still feel guilty when I witness teachers feverishly prepping, planning, resourcing and stressing over a one-hour observation that could chart how smoothly the next 12 months of their career could go. It has become very easy to buy into a system where the outcome of someone peering into a tiny window of practice could provide that teacher with a badge of honour or shame for the foreseeable future; a badge that could lead to promotion and kudos, or something, in some cases quite worryingly, different. For most teachers, observations have always been stressful, but is this process a fair judgement of teachers, and what does it really tell us?

DOI: 10.4324/9781003104698-5

After my first promotion into the world of middle leadership I met an inspirational teacher who helped shine a light on how the *process* was possibly at fault. This teacher wasn't delivering the fashionable, spectacular 'razzmatazz' lessons which I had previously coveted; rather this teacher's super power was 'consistency' – something that up until now had been completely off my radar. This teacher delivered good, solid, purposeful lessons, hour after hour and week after week, which at the time may have been judged as 'satisfactory' to the clipboard-wielding line manager. When some may have been showing a video on the last day of term, this teacher would be teaching a lesson with clear intentions and outcomes and using every last minute of time to ensure the children were learning. What else was clear was that the children not only appreciated and enjoyed the lessons, but their outcomes were the highest in the school.

At this time, I was lecturing to PGCE students on what 'good' and 'outstanding' classroom teaching might look like. I remember sharing examples of marketplace lessons, lauding the idea that we should be teaching different lessons to visual, auditory and kinaesthetic learners, topic work, implicit learning – the list goes on, but deep down I knew that sometimes (not always) 'talk and chalk' and those 'satisfactory' lessons got the results. Then, thanks to the explosion of social media giving access to educational bloggers and thinkers like Tom Sherrington, David Didau, Daisy Christodoulou and John Hattie's meta-analysis of 'Visible Learning,' alongside the changing requirements of the UK national education inspectorate (Ofsted), a question struck me: why was it that sometimes the most quiet, unassuming, old fashioned, least likely to use 'new dynamic techniques' teacher in the school got the best results? We should be asking them how they do it, not recommending ways they should change it.

It was becoming clear that to get the real measure of a teacher and truly understand their impact would take more than an annual observation. Observations were and will continue to be important; the trick would be about taking a holistic view – gathering evidence, triangulating, supporting, nurturing, reviewing and looking for something beyond the razzmatazz.

Transforming practice

If the system isn't broken, why replace it?

My first mainstream assistant headteacher position had responsibility for whole-school teaching and learning. One of my first roles was to review the impact of a particular faculty. I was handed a paper bundle of lesson observations with scrawled writing, numbers and judgements at the bottom. A simple average of the overall grade told me that the faculty was 'good,' but it was clear that this told me nothing about specific strengths and weaknesses, and in terms of setting targets, my opinions were completely subjective. These papers could not help me assure the quality of the faculty nor be used in any meaningful appraisal system. I was reminded of Hattie's work (2012) on how teacher credibility could have such a significant impact on learning, and yet these papers couldn't really tell me anything concrete about the interventions, teaching, learning, credibility or impact of any of the teachers in the faculty.

At the time, Ofsted invited practitioners to meet with the National Director for Schools to talk about the challenges and need for changing how lessons and schools were judged. I came away clear, and more importantly confident, that a handwritten number at the bottom of a two-sided print-out was no longer the way to review a teacher, teaching and impact. The paper system wasn't completely at fault; it was just dated. All the information was available in the school system, but bringing it together was difficult; what was needed was a central format where quality assurance and appraisal evidence could be easily accessed at the touch of a button.

Any school leaders at this point thinking that their system isn't broken, so why replace it, should understand that the system described here can be grown slowly and in conjunction with an existing system. Numbers on the bottom of a sheet do have some merit, but if technology can ease the pressure and eliminate manual triangulation, it can only be a good thing. This system will:

- Save you time
- Put your evidence in one place
- Enable you to share good practice
- Allow you to adapt to research, and most importantly,
- Identify and meet the needs of your school.

Developing a new process

Triangulation is a neat term that we use a lot in education; it sounds simple. It can refer to the process of aligning information, progress with data with teaching or outcomes with behaviour within a year group. It might sound easy, but in practice, finding and sharing the evidence is not.

Microsoft OneNote is a programme or application on many of our computers and laptops. It is usually free to download and can be used on smart phones. Through simple sharing permissions, pages and documents can be accessed, viewed and most importantly edited by others. OneNote allows users to upload pictures, video clips, voice notes and much more: the platform is perfect for triangulating the implicit and explicit variables that might be described as the characteristics of successful teaching.

Step 1

Create a master page/template document. This page should be quick to view and draw together performance data, contextual data, work scrutiny, pupil voice – all accessible via links or pasted directly onto the page. The key is to pull together the evidence that you may later need to triangulate – because the system is completely digital, there really are no limits as to what you can add; but at the start, it should be quite simple.

Step 2

Take the template into the classroom and complete observations directly onto the page: most technology will allow you to take recordings or photographs of good or innovative practice. There is usually an option in the drop-down menu which will automatically paste the clip onto the page, sitting next to any notes that you make. This might include:

- A brief view of the environment (simply take a photograph)
- A reflection on the available data (can be added before the observation)
- What the intentions and intended outcomes are (photograph, description, part of a plan?)
- What the children are learning, whether it links to the curriculum and where
- How resources are used, innovation (maybe a small video clip)
- How feedback is given and how children are assessed.

Step 3

Develop the system. Each teacher grows their own pages with banks of evidence, with teachers and observers adding reflections from other observations.

I quickly began to build a portfolio of what triangulated successful practice looked like – for example where planning was clear, where classroom support staff were well briefed, where resources were ready, where learning episodes were task-focussed, where teaching and questioning were explicit. These characteristics started to point to successful outcomes and engaged children. It also helped unpick where things might not be going so smoothly – why is it that a small group of children are underperforming? A focussed observation on these children might provide evidence that the teacher has simply missed over time. The system paints a picture for you to assure quality. It shows you the evidence, puts it in one place and makes it ubiquitous.

Box 4.1 Examples of comments and photo evidence

Example 1 – feedback notes

This is one of the newest areas of the Academy and looks in good condition. Is there any way that some student work could be displayed on the board outside? We agree it could be more welcoming.

We need to ask ** to remove the boxes. Obviously, a H&S issue.

Example 2 – feedback notes

>   Is there a plan?
>   Is there information and interventions to support CYP?
>   Is it clear what the outcomes are?
>   Are targets identified (specific to learning)?

The planning and organisation was excellent. Context, previous learning, clear outcomes and detailed risk assessment give a clear idea of where, why, what and who these children are. Really impressive. Do you know the learners in this class? Yes, absolutely!

Students are given class outcomes and individual targets.

This is a great way of celebrating individuals. The small notice boards have key words written on them, the class intentions and outcomes are written in books and the star gives an individual target. The clip shows the student knows what his star target is but most importantly understands why. *Start target clip*.

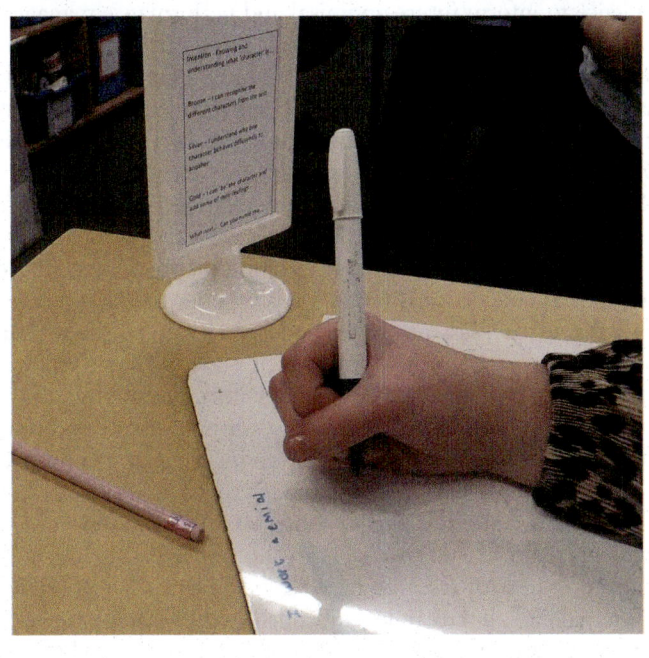

Appraisal and quality assurance 53

Evidence to make accurate judgements

As I moved into headship, the sharing of this platform came into its own. Different people could be part of the process, gathering evidence, reviewing practice and reflecting on the findings. This system can be shared with as few or as many colleagues as you choose, and of course involving teachers in the process of quality assurance is more effective than simply turning up with a clipboard.

As I gathered increasing examples of photographs and video, the OneNote systems linking to Office 365 allowed me to store and produce easily accessible video links to practices that were highly effective – for example, a classroom assistants' behaviour management process for a particularly challenging child or an innovative starter to engage children. These links could be emailed privately to a teacher or shown to a whole staff team (with permission) as part of a CPD session. They were also useful in school improvement meetings or external reviews; if I was asked, "Do teachers promote appropriate discussion about subject matter?" (Ofsted 2019) or the familiar follow-up question of "How do you know?," I was able to provide evidence at the click of a button. I also felt more confident knowing that I had a robust source of evidence to inform future appraisal and performance management conversations, and as sometimes happens, if a teacher does 'freeze' during an observation in unfamiliar circumstances, I had enough evidence to make accurate judgements without being thrown by an anomaly.

An unintended benefit came from the individual feedback sessions between the observed teacher and me (or the line manager). The OneNote system triangulated and demonstrated evidence in front of teachers. There was a clear shift from *me* talking to the *teacher* reviewing the evidence and drawing some of their own (if sometimes guided) conclusions. I was also noticing that in some areas around the school, less attention had been given to the resources, particularly the furniture – so for a teacher to say, "I need to replace those chairs" or "I think those displays look really outdated" can be enormously powerful. The evidence starts to direct and nurture the teachers, rather than the observer giving a 'what I think' view.

I could now confidently judge how effective a faculty was – a process I termed 'judging the faculty footprint.' Adaptations and simple adjustments to the master template can allow observers to look for and keep up to date with research-based good practice. As the system is completely digital, links can be embedded in the master template that can take you directly to the research if it is appropriate. This is not a tool to say, "I told you so," but a tool to learn from and share together.

Learning from the evidence

As the evidence builds and teachers become more confident in the system, it can be used (with caution) to try to discover reasons for possible problems in the classroom or in a faculty. Why are there more behaviour incidents on a certain day at a certain time? It may be that your evidence points to children arriving from other parts of the school at separate times, and so the lesson never starts with the purpose it deserves?

Example 1

Some of our progress data suggested that we had a small group of 15- and 16-year-old girls in an English class who were not achieving. After a small number of observations, we discovered that a classroom assistant was possibly over-supporting the girls and they were becoming too reliant on her: interestingly, it was the classroom assistant (who should be involved in the feedback and reflection process when appropriate) who pointed this out in feedback sessions before the observer had actually noticed.

Example 2

We discovered that a large proportion of the teaching and learning was implicit, and while relationships were good and the children/young people enjoyed the lessons, certain measured outcomes failed to materialise. Teachers didn't always identify issues or practice that needed changes or development. These difficult conversations are always a challenge, but using the system to help those teachers see and join the dots *with you* is an effective way for them to recognise and take ownership of development needs. Linking performance to teacher standards is easier with a bank of accessible evidence; nothing should come as a shock.

Collecting evidence to measure impact

Evidence collection

Evaluating the impact of the system on teachers is essential, and our school has completed some rudimentary research on the process. All observations can be emailed to staff, but when the system works in conjunction with Office 365, the Forms Survey App can be included so that teachers' opinions can be gathered quickly and while observations are fresh in their thoughts. Feedback was collected in three ways:

- First, an anonymous simple questionnaire was emailed to all staff for completion (see Table 4.1 for results).
- Second, a small section of staff was selected at random from senior leadership, middle leadership, and main scale for individual interviews.
- Last, each staff member was asked how the system improved their practice during feedback.

Impact

Teachers

All the teachers returned their questionnaires, and the response was overwhelmingly positive.

The aim of this survey is to review the impact of the use of technology/photographs/video, etc. to provide detailed feedback for lesson observations. Please rate the following:

1. What is your overall view of the system?
2. Does the system provide you with enough feedback to have an impact on your teaching?
3. How disruptive is the observation to your teaching? (Does the observer/equipment get in the way?)
4. Does the system help you plan and use teaching assistants more effectively?
5. Does the system encourage you to think about the environment outside your classroom?
6. Does the system encourage you to think about health and safety in your classroom?
7. Does watching the video clips of other teachers have a positive impact on your own teaching?
8. Do the whole staff feedback sessions using the system have a positive impact on your practice?

Appraisal and quality assurance 57

Table 4.1 Teacher questionnaire (Each bar on the graph identifies positive responses to the 8 questions listed after the table.)

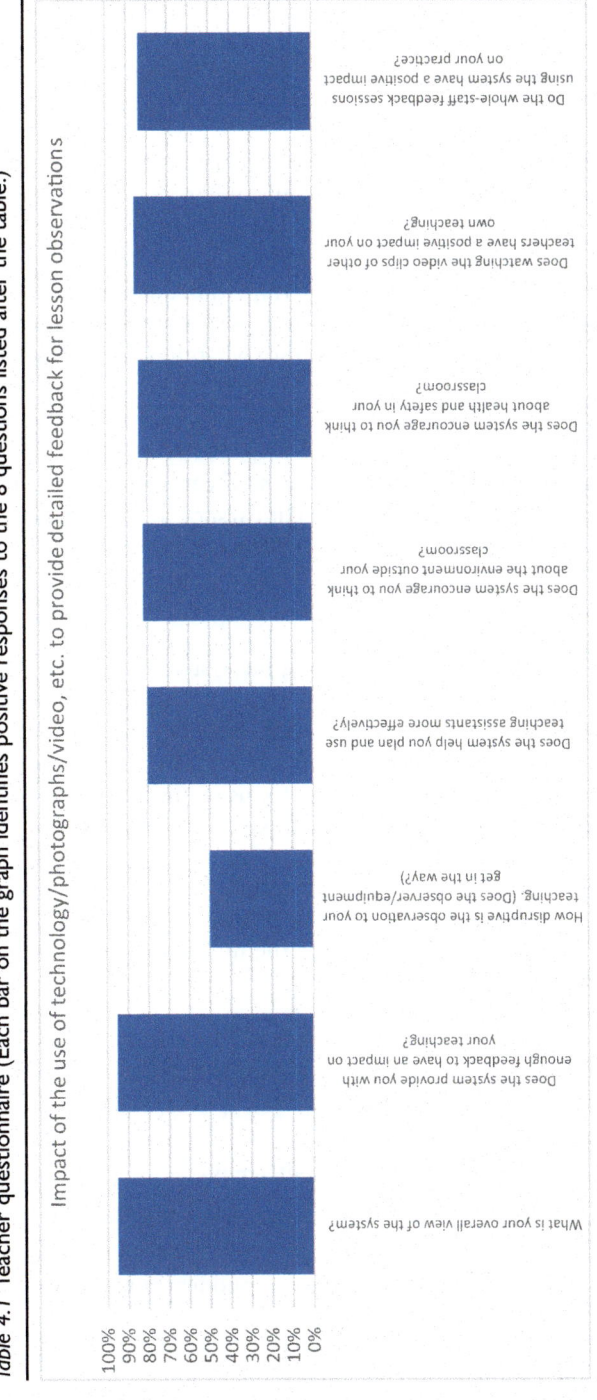

Impact of the use of technology/photographs/video, etc. to provide detailed feedback for lesson observations

Question	Approx. %
What is your overall view of the system?	80%
Does the system provide you with enough feedback to have an impact on your teaching?	80%
How disruptive is the observation to your teaching. (Does the observer/equipment get in the way?)	30%
Does the system help you plan and use teaching assistants more effectively?	70%
Does the system encourage you to think about the environment outside your classroom?	70%
Does the system encourage you to think about health and safety in your classroom?	70%
Does watching the video clips of other teachers have a positive impact on your own teaching?	80%
Do the whole-staff feedback sessions using the system have a positive impact on your practice?	90%

Teachers also gave positive feedback in their interviews:

> It is a good system. It takes some getting used to, but it makes you reflect on your practice.
>
> Videos and photos show the teacher, real time feedback; it's factual and clearly demonstrates what was happening during the observation.
>
> Having feedback in this way is truly clear. Although watching yourself on video takes a bit of getting used to. It allows you to reflect on your practice and helps you see what the observer is seeing.
>
> Videos support judgement by the observer in a tangible way. Annotations on still photos help clarify points made by the observer. Teacher is able to see/hear events/issues/teaching points which were out of sight/earshot at the time. This provides excellent evidence for the teacher to reflect on.

CAUTION

A possible challenge of introducing the system to a school is simply overcoming the fear of change. Having a headteacher in a lesson armed with video/recording/photography equipment in hand can be very off-putting for some, so teachers must feel part of the journey and fully understand a school's justifications for using these techniques. During one of the feedback sessions, a very experienced teacher told me:

> Some staff feel uncomfortable, but do like the opportunity to show the good work they do. Whenever any photos and films are taken, it's a worry where the images go, but staff do trust you and school systems.

I took this as a warning – *never* use this as a tool to show where a teacher is underperforming, and be mindful that these images essentially belong to the person being filmed/photographed.

Teaching and learning and pupil outcomes

The biggest impact was on the accessibility and credibility of evidence for quality assurance and appraisal, but more *important* for me was the improvement in teaching and learning and the increase in pupil outcomes.

In an Ofsted inspection in 2017, the only way that I could demonstrate how effective a teacher might be was to walk the inspector around the school and drop into lessons for a 15-minute observation. It was unfair to the teacher, unrealistic and did not paint an accurate picture. In a follow-up school improvement inspection, where I'd used this system, I had the evidence in front of me. I could demonstrate good practice, and I could triangulate it with performance data. The system gave credibility to our quality assurance, and so I was under the spotlight rather than the teachers (which is the right way round). Our appraisal system is now fully accurate; a teacher's year can be reviewed holistically rather than simply through one lesson observation.

We have seen the quality of teaching and learning move from approximately 60% secure or better to consistently 90% secure or better in three years. Outcomes remain strong but have improved by approximately 10% in a number of subjects. In a recent school review, an Ofsted inspector reported:

> Here I can triangulate your teachers' impact, the sequence of your curriculum and your Academy development priorities. . . . You have enough evidence for a secure judgement to be made.

And on reviewing evidence for a headteacher report on teaching and learning, a trustee said:

> I don't claim to be an expert in teaching; what this provides me with is a window into what teaching in the Academy looks like with a robust commentary to give me the assurances that I need.

Learning, culture, next steps and legacy

The observation should only be a part of the appraisal process. Modernising, evidencing and strengthening this part should help review the whole appraisal process and possibly change the appraisal culture. If there is explicit evidence that performance can be improved at individual or faculty level, then the appraisal process should be linked and used to address those issues. More helpful has been the provision of 'top-down' clarity, enabling senior staff to identify whole-school needs. This year I identified that much of the resourcing and subject knowledge of practitioners was not necessarily being provided and guided by subject leaders; because of this I was able to set whole-academy appraisal targets linked to subject leadership.

The ease of this system to triangulate certainly helps provide evidence, but moving forward I hope that the process will direct me, rather than leave me looking for connections. I now use the same process for well-being checks/interviews for staff and pupils. In the future, I might develop a bank of evidence linking general mood around the Academy and outcomes or discover something completely new that could have a significant impact on the Academy and our leadership and management.

Sustainability needs to be considered. As a member of staff with complete buy-in to the overall achievement of the Academy, it can be easy to assume that everyone else is as committed. Governors and trustees must be aware of the system and policies reviewed where necessary. Training and hardware are also essential – you need hardware that is light, can hold electric charge, can stay logged into your school's Internet connections when you move, can input video and photography, and can link to other systems. You also need to give staff time to use the system; as a headteacher I still have too much ownership of the process and need to build a sustainable legacy.

An unexpected consequence of the system has been its link to classroom management. A number of teachers have noticed personal idiosyncratic traits that appear to help manage classroom behaviour:

- One teacher spotted how their use of body language helped calm down an individual whilst another noticed how she de-escalated and managed a potentially challenging child by adding a short open question followed by a motivational comment and some praise. Both teachers were unaware of these skills and now actively apply them and try to share these with others.
- Some teachers found the photographs and videos useful for spotting where children are pretending to be on task – those who are sometimes experts at 'looking engaged' when actually the second the teacher's back is turned, they start looking out of the window.

Also, being digital, and moving into an ever-virtual world, this system means that meetings and feedback sessions can be held completely online if unexpected circumstances (like the COVID-19 pandemic) dictate.

Recommendations

Recommendations for practice

1 **Get staff on board.** This was not as hard as I thought it might be, but some may remain sceptical of your intentions.

   First, you need to explain the system, clarify your intentions, show examples and help staff recognise that this is a collection of their practices – either with small groups of teachers or whole-staff meetings. This is not a punitive tool. My teachers know that if they are anxious about an observation or teach a lesson that they are disappointed with, I will always have enough evidence to back up their impact on the school.

   Second, show your teachers off – every one of them will have a unique quality, a USP. If you can capture this and share it, staff will learn and grow. I often like to share a photograph or a video clip of some really interesting practice; I find it motivates staff and encourages them to take appropriate risks with their teaching.

2 **Keep on top of the research** to ensure that teachers are aware of the latest interventions and effective practice. Attend Teach meets and keep an eye out for new publications. I once contacted a leading educational blogger and asked him for his top-10 educational best reads. People are often more than happy to help. The best practice might sometimes come when it is least expected, so we should keep an open mind as to *why* this teacher is having such an impact.

3 **Start small**; do not replace the old with the new immediately. Work with, and listen to, the teachers and try to triangulate the aspects that are important to your school first. Don't implement an initiative and use this as a net to catch those not following protocol – show why the initiative is working, demonstrate how it can work with other teachers and support them to make the change.

4 **Share the system with others** in the school. If you have complete ownership, you will miss the expertise of those leaders around you.

5   Try not to use observations more than three times a year. Observations were stressful, and this system can still be stressful. Be clear when the observations are going to be, and don't stay more than 20 minutes unless asked. I find 20 minutes is long enough to gather plenty of information. Be respectful of the effort the teachers have put in, take time writing up the findings and be prepared to change your notes during feedback sessions – we aren't mind-readers, and we can miss things.
6   Finally, and most important, keep an open mind. This tool is to help, not hinder. Go into the lesson observation hoping you will learn something new; remember that lesson observations aren't 'real;' remember their limitations.

Recommended reading

It is essential to stay on top of the research. Use it to inform your own knowledge and link it to practice:

- If you read that effective teaching involves asking a lot of questions to check for understanding in Sherrington and Caviglioli's (2019) 'Rosenshine's principles in action,' then look for questioning when you visit lessons.
- If you read about the 'straw men' in Kirschner and Hendrick's (2020) 'How learning happens' and read that we shouldn't assume that children can multitask, that knowledge *is* important and that the best method to learn is through discovery, then look out for it in your observations.
- Don't fall into the trap of looking for what is fashionable; keep an open mind.

Other useful reads are Daniel Willingham's (2009) 'Why don't children like school?,' Daisy Christodoulou's (2014) 'Seven myths about education' and of course the 'Visible Learning' series by John Hattie. Don't forget, though, that the Internet is rich with research-based good practice – start with the Education Endowment Foundation (EEF) Teaching and Learning Toolkit, and work outwards from there.

References

Christodoulou, D. (2014) *Seven Myths about Education*, London: Routledge

Hattie, J. (2012) *Visible Learning for Teachers: Maximising Impact on Learning*, Abingdon: Routledge

Kirschner, P.A., and Hendrick, C. (2020) *How Learning Happens: Seminal Works in Educational Psychology and What They Mean in Practice*, Abingdon: Routledge

Ofsted (2019) *School Inspection Handbook*, Manchester: Ofsted

Sherrington, T., and Caviglioli, O. (2019) *Rosenshine's Principles in Action*, Suffolk: John Catt Education

Willingham, D.T. (2009) *Why Don't Students Like School? A Cognitive Scientist Answers Questions about How the Mind Works and What It Means for the Classroom*, San Francisco: Jossey-Bass

Chapter 5

Developing whole-school research

Michael Gorton

Context

My school is a larger-than-average primary school with over 450 pupils, located in an ex-mining town in the Midlands. It is two-form entry, taking children from 3–11, and is broadly in line with national averages in relation to pupils with SEN and other characteristics. The school is organised into four phase groups (Early Years, Key Stage 1, Lower Key Stage 2 and Upper Key Stage 2), with each phase covering two-year groups. Each phase is led by a phase leader, with the support of a deputy and assistant headteacher. The school had recently received a successful Ofsted visit where it was rated 'Good,' and the headteacher felt in a position to reflect on current practice to further develop the school.

The school had a history of engaging with professional learning, previously being involved with a local authority project called the Raising Achievement Network, which led to the development of our marking policy. This policy was based around marking in two colours, where staff used green pen to make positive comments and pink pen to challenge, question or ask children to improve a section of work. Within Early Years and Key Stage 1, stamps were used instead of comments to give children more visual prompts in their feedback. The policy had come about as a result of work by three teachers, and then it was rolled out to the whole school.

When the Department for Education (DfE) launched their Workload Challenge research projects, we were keen to be involved, believing it was time to revisit our marking policy. We felt it had become time-consuming, with staff reporting that on average they spent over 12 hours a week marking. This was a school-wide issue and as such, a school-wide solution was needed; so we decided to

DOI: 10.4324/9781003104698-6

think 'big' and involve all teachers in the project. Whilst this was a daunting prospect, it would ensure all year groups were represented and by demystifying the process, help to encourage a research ethos which would continue beyond the project. This was something the headteacher was particularly passionate about, as she wanted to develop staff understanding of how they could carry out research to develop and enhance practice.

Transforming practice

From the outset it was clear this project offered an opportunity to upskill staff and give them an opportunity to develop skills and understanding of the research process. Although our project was part of a larger DfE project on reducing teachers' marking workload without negatively impacting children's achievement, we had flexibility in the way in which we designed and delivered it. This gave us an opportunity to learn not just about marking but also about the mechanics of successfully running a whole-school project.

We were keen to make use of existing literature about research within the classroom and felt this needed to be shared with staff. Using Hattie's 'Visible Learning Impact Cycle' (Hattie *et al.* 2016) as a starting point (see Recommended Reading), we began to discuss ways to maintain student outcomes whilst reducing workload. This resulted in a project that aimed to improve the effectiveness of marking and open staff's eyes to the impact of feedback as a whole (rather than just marking). It was important to design the project to encourage teachers to shape how this looked rather than relying on a predetermined approach being applied from above. There were two key strands to this approach:

I UNPICKING THE PROBLEMS

Whilst it was widely acknowledged that marking was a significant workload issue (Gibson *et al.* 2015), we needed clarity about *why* this was the case in our school in order to address it. We wanted to know teachers' thoughts about marking and how they perceived it, so we had an accurate picture before designing our project. To achieve this, we carried out a staff survey. We also wanted to know where problems may arise. One issue identified was the feeling that marking had become a task for people other than the children

(SLT, Ofsted, parents). Knowing there was work to be done around the purpose of marking before we started ensured that a potential stumbling block – teacher fear of outsider judgement – did not impact on the project.

2 GETTING EVERYONE INVOLVED

It has been noted that developing teacher empowerment and collective decision-making forms an important part of school leadership (Saleh and Khine 2014), and this view fit well with that of our leadership team, who wanted to develop teachers' understanding of an evidence-based approach, so they knew not just *what* we do but *why*. We decided to hand ownership to teachers to avoid the feeling that the project was being 'done to' them and to encourage a more participatory approach: it was their workload we wanted to reduce, so who better to have an input on those changes? We began by asking staff to review and evaluate current practice and consider changes they could make to reduce workload without negatively impacting on pupil progress. By giving staff ownership of their part of the project, we wanted to encourage engagement and develop a more research-based mindset, which would have an impact long after this research was completed.

Our new approaches

The new approaches decided upon were dependent on the needs identified by teachers in each year group, but they all showed the reflective and evaluative approach which we had been so keen to inculcate in staff. Although each year group was able to come up with its own approach to marking, there were many commonalities in approach. In younger year groups there was an acknowledgement that many comments used previously simply weren't for the children to read – so Early Years and Key Stage 1 staff decided to move away from written comments towards more instant feedback, and Key Stage 1 decided that photos provided evidence of learning themselves and did not require additional comments.

Our previous approach of using pink and green pens was also scrapped across the school, with some year groups trialling using different prescribed colours, and others deciding that any colour could now be used. A key thread which ran across all the trials was about reducing the quantity of teacher comments and marking, with a shift particularly in Key Stage 2 classes towards giving more ownership to the pupils themselves. This could be seen through increased use of peer marking where appropriate and through changing expectations – the old approach where teachers provided pupils with spelling corrections shifted so that pupils were now encouraged to use dictionaries to correct the spellings which were now simply highlighted by the teacher. This subtle shift in expectations was hoped to both engage children more in the process and reduce the time spent marking by teachers.

Collecting evidence to measure impact

Evidence collection

We needed staff views at the start and end of the project so that we could measure the impact of the changes, but we also wanted the project to encourage ongoing reflection and to give us students' perspectives, so we collected evidence in the following ways:

- To get a baseline of existing marking workload, teachers completed an online survey before the project began, where they were asked to identify the amount of time spent on marking each week, as well as the factors influencing this.
- Once the new feedback policies began, 'pupil comment' boxes were introduced in Years 2–6.
- To encourage ongoing reflection, teachers were given a journal. Time was set aside at the start of each staff meeting for them to reflect on the project over the previous week and record any thoughts/positives/negatives. Initially this required prompts, with questions to think about, but soon staff became confident in structuring their own reflections.
- Partway through the project, the teachers split into phases (EYFS and KS1, lower KS2, upper KS2) to form focus groups with an opportunity to discuss the project thus far, covering:
  - What was working well
  - Any issues raised
  - How it linked back to the project aims.
- At the end of the project, groups of children from all year groups were interviewed by the project leader about their views on marking.

- At the end of the project, staff completed a follow-up survey to provide a comparison of their original views and experiences of marking.

In order to ensure that our research approach was ethical, we followed BERA guidelines (2018), and informed consent was sought from the children and their parents. At the design stage, a letter was sent out to all parents explaining our proposals and giving them the right to opt out on their child's behalf. Out of 474 pupils, only one opted out.

Impact

Impact on workload

In terms of the aims of the project, it was a success for staff from Year 2 to Year 6, who noticed a difference in their workload, many significantly. Key changes noted by both staff and the headteacher included:

- Less time marking
- More time to focus on the fun delivery and resourcing of lessons
- More free time
- Staff leaving school at an appropriate time and doing more leisure activities.

One teacher commented: "It's amazing what we thought we needed to be doing, when actually we were just wasting time" (KS2 Teacher). However, staff in FS1-Year 1 felt that the changes had less impact, as marking formed less of their workload. It was important that we acknowledged both experiences of the project, and it was hoped that the research ethos developed would encourage the FS1-Year 1 staff to consider other areas of practice they could investigate in order to reduce their workload.

Teachers' views: survey

Staff were asked to complete a survey to establish the effect of marking on workload. By gathering this information before making changes, we identified a baseline and highlighted some of the underlying causes behind it. Returning to the same questions at the end, we were able to see what impact the changes had led to, giving us a clear understanding of how marking workload had changed. At the end of the project respondents commented that workload was "much more manageable compared to the old policy" (KS2 Teacher 1), and as a result they had more free time, commenting that:

I've finally had time to join the gym. (KS2 Teacher 2)

It's made a lot of difference to workload. (KS2 Teacher 4)

I can't remember the last time I had to take books home. (KS2 Teacher 5)

The positive impact of the project on workload highlighted the success of handing an element of control in the design to the teachers. As the experts in their classroom, they were able to design and implement changes which worked for them and their children.

Teachers' views: research journals

Teachers were given weekly reflection time; they were encouraged to note down thoughts about positives, negatives, any comments from children or feelings they had. Initially this required prompts from the project leader with questions that staff should think about, but soon staff were able to structure and formulate their own thoughts, with some developing questions on which they wanted to follow up.

The journals acted as a fantastic resource when evaluating the project, with the weekly recordings ensuring that thoughts and impressions throughout the project were not lost or forgotten over time. Looking through, you could see how staff had gone from 'feeling very guilty/lazy' at the beginning of the project to noting after several months that: "Marking less is saving lots of time. Children's performance has not been impacted" (KS2 Teacher). Use of journals, and dedicating a small amount of staff meeting time to their use, also meant that the project maintained momentum and remained visible. Crucially, teachers were reflecting on *why* they marked and how they could change their own practises to ensure that feedback was meaningful. This growth in self-reflection was seen as particularly positive in light of our aim of developing a research ethos across school.

Teachers' views: focus group

Partway through the project, the teachers split into phases (EYFS and KS1, Lower KS2 and Upper KS2) to form focus groups to discuss the project, covering:

- What was working well
- Any issues raised
- How it linked back to the project aims.

To ensure that staff had the opportunity for reflection and discussion, a staff meeting was set aside for the focus groups. This meant that staff didn't have to 'find' the time to discuss the project and also highlighted the value being placed on research.

These discussions informed our next steps for developing marking and feedback. Independence of children was highlighted as an issue, with 9/15 teachers viewing independence as a positive element that required further development. One KS2 teacher commented, "They're getting better at independent feedback; they just need more training." Teachers also highlighted the need to work on basic skills, like dictionary work, so this focus on independence translates into more effective feedback for children. By using the focus groups in this way, we encouraged our teachers to reflect critically on their project and identify their learning.

The impact on the children

Interviews and feedback showed children had mixed views about marking, in much the same way that they had done with the previous approach. For some the increased independence was a negative: "It's harder, I have to find my spellings in a dictionary now" (KS2 Child), whilst others enjoyed this challenge: "You have to look up the spellings, it's harder but better" (KS2 Child). It was important that these views were shared with staff to provide some perspective. One teacher noted: "We'd trained them to expect us to do all the thinking for them," highlighting that staff were analysing the responses of children to the changes. Most important, staff and pupils agreed changes had not had a detrimental impact on progress.

Children's interviews

At the end of the project, we compared the children and the teachers' views about the changes. Children from each year group were interviewed by the project leader, offering a mixture of opinions. There was a link between whether the growth of independence was perceived as a positive or negative by the children and whether they liked or disliked the new marking: children either enjoyed being challenged by having to think more, commenting things like, "I like to work out what I need to improve – it's a challenge" (Year 5 Child), or they missed the old way where corrections were done for them, saying, "It's harder because you have to look up the spellings" (Year 4 Child). In Year 1, this split was between boys and girls: the boys apparently liked being made to think; the girls did not.

'Pupil comment' box

Comment boxes were introduced in Years 2–6. It was quickly identified these weren't being used, so each class set aside time when children could share their views. Children were given self-adhesive notes to record their thoughts, although younger children had a whole-class discussion with the teachers scribing. These comments gave a clear indication of pupil thoughts about the changes to marking and helped us to evaluate the impact of changes.

Conclusions

It was clear that the project had a positive impact on workload for staff working in Year 2 to Year 6. On completion, there was no negative impact on results, suggesting the project had met its aim of reducing workload without negatively impacting on pupil outcomes.

In terms of the wider impact, going whole-school meant that a greater number of staff participated in the project than on previous occasions and were therefore able to develop research skills. One teacher commented that taking part in the project was "a great experience that has had a big impact on my well-being and helped me to reflect more on what I do" (KS2 Teacher). This increase in reflection and a greater understanding of evidence-gathering has become more visible in teachers' practice since the project ended, with the practice of getting a baseline seen across a range of initiatives (especially in the design of staff CPD), so that impact is measurable.

Ethical considerations were also something that took some thought when designing the project; we knew that pupil views were important to give balance to our conclusions, but it was important we were mindful of the ethics of involving children in research. We had parental consent to talk to children about the project, but we also ensured that any contributions from children were anonymous and that children knew their participation was optional. It was important that staff understood this was an issue of ethics, so it was always made clear when discussing the collection of pupil views how they could opt out. This was easier in younger year groups, where feedback was gathered through class discussion, but it was still achieved in older year groups through the use of anonymous feedback on self-adhesive notes which allowed children to write nothing if they chose to.

Going whole-school was not without its issues, especially with the differing expectations and abilities of the children involved. It took time to ensure that staff understood the project wasn't about everyone doing the same thing – it was about them approaching the project in the same way, but adapting for their age/stage. This was when the regular reflection time and ongoing interest in staff voice was particularly effective, as it meant that issues were being identified and responded to throughout. It was important that this was the case for all staff, and (knowing some would find this difficult) we tried to remove barriers to participation by setting aside time for these activities. As a result, all staff participated fully and ensured that children within their classes did so as well.

Recommendations

Recommendations for practice

As a result of running our research project we learnt the following:

1 Trust the staff

Teachers are the experts within their own classrooms; by giving staff the power to affect their own change, we found a wide variety of strategies being trialled and an enthusiasm for the research project which we had not seen previously. Whilst not every change was incorporated into our feedback and marking policy, staff could see that they had all contributed to it. This was powerful and meant that there was a greater understanding of not just what we did, but why we did it that way.

2 Have a clear project outline

Having a clear outline of the project which we could share with staff from the beginning was crucial to developing staff understanding. We had just over a term to carry out the research, so it was important that everyone was clear on what would happen and when to ensure that we fitted each aspect in. This also meant that staff were aware of when key data collection points would be, so they could ensure they were fully prepared.

3 Be explicit about what you are doing and why

It was important that staff knew what we were doing and when, but they also needed to understand *why* we were doing it. By giving staff clarity over the purpose of each step, they were confident about how to deliver it. For example, when introducing the project and beginning with a staff survey, it needed to be clear this would form the baseline against which the performance of the project would be judged, so candid responses were required.

4 Be explicit about the expectations and aims

Staff clarity about the aims and outcomes of any project is crucial. One of the issues we came across early on was that staff would talk about how they could make changes for the benefit of the children, which was not the stated aim of the project. We had to be clear that whilst teacher instinct may tell us to make changes which we feel will impact on students, the aim of the project was to reduce workload. As long as the changes didn't lead to a decrease in pupil outcomes, the changes would be acceptable. This took a while to embed within staffs' minds, but regular reassurance from the headteacher was helpful, and we were vindicated in this approach when statutory assessments showed there had not been a drop in pupil performance following the project.

5 Know your starting point – using evidence

We knew that marking was a big workload issue, but we weren't entirely sure why. In order to plan the project effectively we had to know people's thoughts, so we used a survey to find out what staff thought about the current marking policy. We needed staff to be honest, so we made the survey anonymous in order to get the most accurate responses. Once we had the responses, we looked for patterns and considered whether there were any potential problems raised. This was particularly important because it allowed us to identify a perception amongst staff that marking was for groups other than the children, which we then addressed.

6 Build in ongoing reflection

Reflective journals were introduced, and time was given in every staff meeting to encourage discussion and reflection on the impact of changes staff members had made, both on themselves and on their students. This ongoing reflection not only encouraged staff to notice the impact of their changes, but we saw staff starting to discuss and implement further changes independently.

Recommended reading

Burton, D., and Bartlett, S. (2005) *Practitioner Research for Teachers*, London: Sage
This provides a good introduction to carrying out practice based research, we found this especially useful in the planning stage.

Hattie, J. (2012) *Visible Learning for Teachers*, London: Routledge
This provides research based insights into feedback from both child and teacher perspectives, which helped us to critique existing approaches.

Hattie, J., Masters, D., and Birch, K. (2016) *Visible Learning into Action: International Case Studies of Impact*, London: Routledge

Pages 10 and 11 outline a five-step improvement cycle (summarised here) based on Hattie's research, which we used to form the basis of our research approach:

1 Identify student needs.
2 What do staff need to make this happen?
3 What needs to change to make this happen?
4 What is the impact of these changes?
5 Review outcomes and decide where to go next.

References

British Educational Research Association (BERA) (2018) *Ethical Guidelines for Educational Research*, London: BERA

Gibson, S., Oliver, L., and Dennison, M. (2015) *Workload Challenge: Analysis of Teacher Consultation Responses*, London: DFE

Hattie, J., Masters, D., and Birch, K. (2016) *Visible Learning into Action: International Case Studies of Impact*, London: Routledge

Saleh, I.M., and Khine, M.S. (2014) *Reframing Transformational Leadership: New School Culture and Effectiveness*, Rotterdam: Sense Publishers

Chapter 6

What are you waiting for? Get your school Poverty Proofed

Breaking the cycle of disadvantage

Chris Wardle

Context

There are approximately 4.2 million children living in poverty in the UK today, which is around 30% of all children there (Institute for Fiscal Studies 2020). In some areas, like mine (Blackpool), this number is even higher, with 35% of children living in poverty. This is not set to improve, as forecasts suggest that by 2022, 5.2 million children in the UK will be living in poverty, the highest since modern record-keeping began (Social Mobility Commission 2020).

In schools, poverty is often associated with children and young people in receipt of free school meals (FSM) and pupil premium (PP) funding. While this is a superficially useful indicator, we know that many children and young people trapped in poverty are not eligible for, or in receipt of, FSM or PP; these are what I consider as the 'ghost poor' – unlabelled, but living in destitution. As a result, Poverty Proofing at my high school utilises a broader definition of poverty that seeks to understand the ways in which poverty is experienced at school and how it restricts pupils' opportunities to flourish. We recognise that being in the grip of poverty means that children and their parents have to go without things that everyone should be able to have in a decent society.

Currently, our economy is locking families into poverty by restricting their options and presenting them with impossible decisions, such as choosing between heating their homes and putting food on the table. 70% of children living in poverty are in a household where at least one parent works, largely because low-paying, temporary, or insecure jobs are often not enough to provide a sufficient income (Social Mobility Commission 2020). Combined with rising living costs, a lack of affordable housing and ongoing reforms

DOI: 10.4324/9781003104698-7

to the benefits system means that families face difficult situations and are restricted in their ability to access basic amenities and participate in social life.

In my experience, a high percentage of disadvantaged children have lower attendance, more challenging behaviour and make less progress compared to non-disadvantaged children. The common link between these children is poverty. They have little income in their household. The way in which we can 'break the cycle' of poverty as educators is to ensure that we do all we can to address any in-school barriers that may disadvantage those already disadvantaged, to ensure that the educational progress and pastoral growth of our disadvantaged pupils is equal to that of their more affluent peers.

At our school, senior leaders researched how the work of Children North East and their Poverty Proofing programme could help us get a more accurate picture of poverty from our own community voice. We sought to use the information to ensure that our policies and procedures were not further disadvantaging our disadvantaged pupils. In this chapter, I will explore how the Children North East's Poverty Proofing programme has influenced our school and our wider family of schools in the North West within our Multi-Academy Trust.

What is poverty?

Before 'Poverty Proofing' is undertaken within any setting, staff (including senior leaders), must review what poverty truly is. Prejudice is formed around poverty, and alarmingly, people are often quick to judge about:

1 The person who is claiming benefit but buying alcohol or smoking cigarettes
2 The person whose children are without food but wear the latest trainers
3 The person who works three jobs, has little food, but has Sky TV

The inner voice of some reading this chapter may feel strongly about these views, but for this chapter and as a school leader, we have to put these to one side and consider what poverty really is for some; this may challenge thinking. In essence, that's exactly what Poverty Proofing does – it challenges thinking.

People with expendable income take things for granted: the general household bills like utilities, mortgage or rent, food, clothing, car fuel and maintenance. Then, there's budgeting of your expendable income for 'fun stuff' like restaurants, entertainment and the 'because presents' for children. People who are poor, who live below the breadline, cannot budget. They cannot afford the general household bills for utilities, rent and food. The ends do not meet. Those who are poor must go without things that others take for granted – as a YouGov survey (Sustain 2018) identified:

- 23% of parents skipped a meal because they couldn't afford to eat while their children ate.
- 8% of adults go an entire day without eating because they cannot afford to eat.

The Trussell Trust (2020) also reported that 1.9 million food parcels had been distributed in the 12 months prior to March 2020, and during the COVID-19 pandemic, approximately 2,600 have been donated *every day* to children.

The impact of poverty

Being without enough money to live manifests in different ways. The British Medical Association (2017) describes how poverty can increase prevalence of chronic illnesses and mental ill health and how it can reduce life expectancy. Poverty can also harm children's education through lower engagement, attendance and attainment, reducing their educational outcomes and future life opportunities (Office for National Statistics 2020).

It is hard to empathise with someone who is impoverished if you have never been impoverished. However, what is remarkable is that there are many teachers and leaders out there like me, who were once an 'FSM pupil.' Maybe we just want to give back.

'Poverty Proofing'

Poverty Proofing is quite simply the most powerful piece of school voice that I have ever seen. It involves questioning pupils, parents, teachers, associate staff and governors to get the voice of the school on practices from attendance to trips and visits. The questions are skilfully written to ascertain the view of poverty during the school day from each stakeholder. Poverty Proofing is a wonderful process that will challenge the school – focussing the school to question stakeholders through the lens of poverty, to direct the leadership team's focus and help to create a more even platform for disadvantaged learners. Poverty Proofing highlights the disadvantages of the school day upon disadvantaged pupils – disadvantages that no school leader intentionally creates, but disadvantages that creep into a school or become a part of the school culture. To recognise these (and change the school culture) creates a more level playing field and a place where disadvantaged pupils may thrive.

Transforming practice

Poverty Proofing our school

The process

I first heard about Poverty Proofing – a programme developed by Children North East – through the CEO of our Multi-Academy Trust and my headteacher. After contacting Luke Bramhall (Poverty Proofing Co-ordinator and Participation Service Manager at Children North East) to discover more, we decided to engage with the process, as we could clearly see the benefits for our community. Supported by Children North East, we used the following process, to carry out a Poverty Proofing audit.

1 Luke Bramhall became our Poverty Proofing Lead. He came into school and trained 20 peer researchers (Year 10 pupils) for half a day, covering:

- Poverty and Poverty Proofing, taking them through what poverty actually is and their perceptions of poverty, challenging their thinking.
- The rationale of questions and examples of typical responses. He explained how to limit their input and focus on gathering interview responses from the children.
- The need for anonymity and confidentiality, the moral principles of ethical research – they were told not to discuss their findings or share the names of any anonymised interview responses with anyone outside of the research group to ensure an ethical process (unless an individual's response raised concern that required passing onto the safeguarding team).

2 Luke provided a keynote to all staff on what poverty was and what Poverty Proofing looked like.

3   Luke and the peer researchers interviewed all pupils in the school.
    - A timetable was created so that the same children were not quizzed throughout the day. Each researcher had their own timetable to follow. Teachers and support staff were aware of this timetable and expected children to arrive.
    - Three Year 10 peer researchers went into a classroom, the children were split into three groups, and each researcher took one group through a line of questioning.
    - The questions dug deep into the school day, its policies and procedures – for example, attendance and behaviour were questioned in depth to discover what children thought of those policies and procedures.
4   Luke and the peer researchers spent time with pupils during all aspects of the school day, including gathering information at breakfast club, break time, lunchtime and after school clubs. Eating dinner with the pupils and asking questions around school meals was a revelation; it became apparent how some children just do not have enough to eat and are hungry inside and outside of school. Children were honest and divulged information about empty cupboards at home and their living conditions. The line of questioning did not tackle home poverty issues; but in my experience, children will tell you a lot more than what the question asks.
5   All parents and carers, staff and governors were sent electronic questionnaires devised by Children North East (a hard copy could be requested). The questions for these groups were similar to those asked of the pupils, requesting opinions on topics like rewards, sanctions, trips and food – a full list of categories can be seen under the next sub-section, 'What we discovered.' Completed questionnaires were returned to the school anonymously. These were reviewed and analysed by the Poverty Proofing Lead and summarised within a written report.
6   A selection of parents, associate staff, teaching staff, leaders and governors were interviewed by the Poverty Proofing Lead. They were sent a letter, asking for volunteers, but as the number of positive responses was relatively small, all who volunteered were interviewed. Separate appointments were made with staff so that specific questions could be asked – for example:
    - The Business Manager was asked about how payment for school trips operated.

- Teachers were asked whether money was collected for charity and if so, how?
- The site manager was asked about non-uniform days – whether there was a difference between how pupils are presented in uniform compared to non-uniform.

7   Luke Bramhall wrote the draft findings and final report (with suggested actions). These were sent to the school as amendable documents.

General process issues

Stakeholder views were given anonymously in order to try and capture an honest view. If there was a safeguarding concern, normal school safeguarding procedures were followed. Pupils were told prior to questioning about what topics would have to be passed on to the school safeguarding team if they surfaced. Peer researchers were not trained in safeguarding but were told to make a note of the name of the pupil and the query if anything came up in conversation that they were unsure of – these queries would be discussed with the school safeguarding team.

All of this research evidence was gathered and analysed for the final report by the Poverty Proofing Lead. A discussion on the draft findings amongst senior leaders challenged existing thinking and clarified information gathered during the process. (Peer researchers were not involved in this process, but on reflection, I can't think of a reason why they couldn't be a part of it.) This culminated in an action plan, drafted from the initial findings and the Poverty Proofing final report. (It made little sense to wait for the final report to come through, when the school could act on some initial findings almost immediately.)

This feedback process can feel slightly uncomfortable, as some of the findings are so blatantly obvious that you wonder why you hadn't addressed such issues in the first place. For example, our report showed that:

- The allocation of free school meal funding was placed on the accounts of eligible pupils at 12:00 p.m. This meant that, unlike their peers, children in receipt of FSM could only use their money at lunchtime. They had no eligibility to use this funding at break time. The headteacher rectified this immediately so that they had the right to spend their money at break time as well as lunchtime. The impact of this was almost immediate;

they could access their allowance earlier in the day, eating when they choose like their peers: we were levelling the playing field through a simple action.
- The colour of our blazer in Year 11 is different from the rest of the school. Our audit identified that children and parents questioned this culture as it was an additional cost to the family for only nine months of wear. We have now thought through our uniform policy and are slowly introducing a new standardised uniform.
- There were 40 pupils not accessing their entitlement to free school meals. When we phoned parents, some were unaware that their children were on FSM, or they assumed that their child was on FSM, but the child was not aware. Through a phone call, this was rectified, and children were accessing the funds that they were entitled to.

Some of the findings may cut against and challenge your thinking. You have to be prepared for that. Pupil voice and community voice make up the report – that is what makes this process so important.

What we discovered

The findings were split into the following categories:

- **Behaviour, reward and attendance** – we found that we were sanctioning pupils in receipt of PP funding for behaviour and punctuality more than any other demographic group.
- **Bullying** – we found that our systems and processes were robust and that children felt well supported.
- **Careers** – pupils and parents commended us for our careers programme, which starts in Year 7 and continues throughout the school; it isn't a 'quick chat' in Year 11.
- **Charity fundraising and community** – a sizeable minority of pupils and parents didn't like non-uniform days. We had already banned non-uniform days, and pupils still supported this decision.
- **Curriculum and ability groups** – food technology came out as an area to review for pupils receiving PP; access was an issue because of the cost of ingredients.
- **Extra-curricular** – pupils and parents felt that we supported them well when they needed assistance to pay for trips and visits.
- **Food** – there were some issues with pupil premium (see earlier discussions).
- **Homework** – pupil access to a learning hub where homework can be conducted was a big success with our pupils.

- **Leadership and governance** – we had a really good awareness of the impact of poverty. This is probably because I went on a training course a few months prior to our audit and we had already acted on some areas.
- **Resources** – we did not ask for many additional resources, and parents really liked this. We provided planners, jotters, knowledge organisers, stationary, etc.
- **Support to parents and families** – 90% of parents felt that we did support them and didn't ask for money for their children.
- **Transport** – most pupils walked or cycled to school, so transportation wasn't really something that impacted family expenditure.
- **Uniform** – see earlier discussion.
- **Well-being and mental health** – we learnt that we could do more for children experiencing mental health issues, so we have now appointed two mental health workers.
- **Other** (areas of the report that required further exploration) – children could tell who had money and who didn't, especially when wearing their own clothes. However, this was less apparent in school since we abolished non-uniform day.

Action

Our school audit took six days to complete, and the subsequent report was comprehensive. 'What we discovered' shows only some examples of the many findings. As a senior leadership team, we created a strategy to implement key findings of the report. We looked at the 'low-hanging fruit' and acted swiftly on those things that we could implement almost immediately, putting a longer-term strategy in place with milestones on other areas.

An example of 'low-hanging fruit' was that raising money for charity caused embarrassment for some pupils when they didn't have their £1 donation. We immediately abolished collecting money for charity and switched to charity awareness. Longer-term strategies like changing the style of uniform may take up to five years to embed, and our uniform will look a 'out of sorts' for some time, but we know that our strategy has Poverty Proofing in mind.

Two years on, we are still working through areas of the report. Our disadvantaged data P8 was −0.67 three years ago. In 2019, it was −0.18 (0.22 above national average disadvantaged data), and the data for 2020 has continued this trajectory, producing a positive P8.

I am not suggesting that our Poverty Proofing developments were solely responsible for this year-on-year improvement trend. Many factors contributed – most importantly, great leadership and great quality teaching. I *am* suggesting that the process of Poverty Proofing and the understanding of what poverty really means has left a long-lasting impression on the leadership decisions made by the school. This means that the impoverished young people of our community get a better deal at school because of this, providing another platform to close the 'disadvantage gap' and move towards equality in terms of outcomes, broadening life chances and life choices. We hope to provide children with a brighter future, a future where they are more likely to be accepted into Level 3 courses of their choosing. Being told you cannot access specific courses because of poor qualifications must be soul-destroying. The aspiration of our community is that all children will compete with the best of the local area regardless of background, that they can access future courses and that they do have options.

Poverty Proofing development across the Trust

The Trust CEO's vision was for all schools within the Trust 'family' to be Poverty Proofed, so senior and middle leaders across the Trust were trained about poverty, Poverty Proofing and auditing. In most cases, the leaders had some responsibility for pupil premium. The training took two days. Those trained shadowed my school's audit and took on a strand of questioning and interviewing pupil groups. Following this, we set about auditing the other Trust schools, all of which were primary schools. We did this 'in house' as we now had the expertise to carry out the audit ourselves. We found that an audit of a primary school with a one-form intake can take approximately two days, and it could take three days for a two-form intake. Our audit reports were sent to Luke and his team at Children North East for quality assurance before they were issued to the Trust's schools. Schools received their own bespoke reports, which had a similar structure to that of my high school and had been reviewed prior to being finalised.

Collecting evidence to measure impact

The impact of our Poverty Proofing development has been nothing short of phenomenal.

Evidence collection

Approximately one year following the audit report, I sent out to the headteachers of the Trust a form requesting specific evidence from their strategic plan of the impact of Poverty Proofing that was implemented from the report.

Impact

These are some of the outcomes described by the headteachers of our nine schools:

> We have noticed an improvement in the consistency of the behaviour system and its use across all staff. Children are clear about the system.

> Attendance has raised significantly in one year. School cumulative attendance was 88%. It is now 92.5%. The report suggested that the boys with pupil premium in particular lacked a significant male figure. We employed a male youth worker and changed our curriculum, and attendance of these boys improved significantly.

> If we raise money, we only ask for a donation where no set amount is requested. This has significantly increased attendance on charitable days.

> We no longer collect money for charity, rather we raise awareness. Our parents have given really positive feedback as some didn't have the money to give.

> Year groups have been placed on a rota at lunchtimes so that all year groups have a day in which they are first in the queue. Children's ideas of what they want has been incorporated into the menu.

> We now schedule payments for trips around paydays and give longer notice of payment schemes.

> We have produced a plan for parents and carers of when additional money is asked for. We have used our sports premium budget to subsidise all sports trips and activities.

> We no longer question children if money has not been paid, but rather we only speak to the parents or carers.

We have installed a 'bring and swap' clothing rail. Not only are school uniforms placed on the rail but coats, shoes, trainers, football boots, bags, etc. Our parents have welcomed the idea and are using it a lot.

We no longer ask for money at the school fayre. Rather, the children buy a book of five tickets and can use those tickets for any of the stalls, e.g. face painting.

We have sourced a new school photographer who is less expensive, and the packages of photos are much cheaper.

We don't ask for any contributions towards model making in school, and we do not set any homework where making models is required.

We ask parents and carers not to send in items if it's their child's birthday; rather, we celebrate them in class.

World Book Day is now an opportunity for children to make costumes from the materials we provide. We ask that parents and carers do not go and buy the latest costumes from stores.

Wider impact

Poverty Proofing our policies and procedures has been a tremendous success. Overall school attendance has improved, behaviour has improved, and outcomes have improved across the Trust schools. Again, this is not solely down to Poverty Proofing the Trust's schools, but it has been a contributing factor towards their success. Every school within the Trust has been graded at least Ofsted 'Good' since we carried this out. A section of our school's report (March 2019) read:

> Leaders have an accurate understanding of the school's strengths and any areas needing further attention, which helps them to plan improvements effectively. For example, when senior leaders spotted the previously high number of fixed-term exclusions for disadvantaged pupils, which contributed to these

pupils' weak progress, they took swift action. This has made a significant difference to these pupils' success at the school. They are now supported to behave well and make good progress.

Within the academic year 2020–2021 to date, there has been no fixed-term exclusion of any disadvantaged pupils, or indeed any pupils, at our school. This improvement of behavioural outcomes is due to many factors; the most important factor is a shift in school culture academically and pastorally.

Poverty Proofing has become an ever-present part of our DNA. We challenge ourselves in our decision making, ensuring that we place poverty firmly at the forefront of our strategies so that we level the playing field as much as possible within our school. This has had an impact on the culture of the school, where decisions are not made without thinking of the impact on our impoverished pupils.

The future

Ideally, the Trust would have completed a Poverty Proofing exercise of one strand of the report in each of the Trust schools in late June/early July of 2020 had it not been for the COVID-19 factor. We now aim to engage with a Poverty Proofing strand within one another's schools in 2021 and complete a full audit of each school in 2022–2023.

Implementing Poverty Proofing is not something that occurs as a 'one off' and shelved for the report to gather dust. It is a continual process, a process that is weaved into all aspects of school leadership and becomes the responsibility of all leaders. We owe it to every child to provide the very best learning opportunity each day.

Recommendations

1   Explore what poverty is. You will need to challenge the preconceived ideas about poverty that may dwell within you and the people you are surrounded by. A good starting point is to read Mazzoli Smith, L., and Todd, L. (2016) *Poverty Proofing the School Day: Evaluation and Development Report*, Newcastle upon Tyne: Newcastle University Research Centre for Learning and Teaching.

2 **Understand that Poverty Proofing EYFS is a challenge.** I'm a secondary school teacher and leader with only a week of primary school experience while on teacher training 20 years ago. When I audited EYFS, I made many mistakes. One of our primary headteachers adapted the Poverty Proofing questions through play. This proved to be a huge success and allowed EYFS children a voice in their report findings.

3 **Be prepared for some findings that will cut against your perceptions of your school.** When they are delivered, don't respond immediately. Rather, reflect on what is said and then think about how you are going to tackle the issues that are raised.

4 **Be mindful that the report can throw up anomalies.** For example, one child may think something about rewards, but that will not be representative of the school population. However, it might actually be important and relevant, so it's always worth considering all points raised. A challenge of the final report is to mention the frequency with which something is raised.

5 **Reach out to www.povertyproofing.co.uk.** Ask which schools have been involved with the Poverty Proofing programme near you. Starting a dialogue with neighbouring schools about their experiences may prove to be really beneficial for your 'Poverty Proofing journey.'

References

British Medical Association (2017) *Reducing the Impact of Poverty: A Briefing from the Board of Science 2017.* Available online at: www.bma.org.uk/media/2084/health-at-a-price-2017.pdf (Accessed 29/01/21)

Institute for Fiscal Studies (2020) *Living Standards, Poverty and Inequality in the UK: 2020.* Available online at: www.ifs.org.uk (Accessed 09/01/21)

Office for National Statistics (2020) *Child Poverty and Education Outcomes by Ethnicity.* Available online at: www.ons.gov.uk (Accessed 29/01/21)

Social Mobility Commission (2020) *Monitoring Social Mobility 2013–2020: Is the Government Delivering on Our Recommendations?* London: Social Mobility Commission

Sustain (2018) *1 in 4 UK Parents Skipping Meals Due to Lack of Money.* Available online at: www.sustainweb.org (Accessed 08/01/21)

Trussell Trust (2020) *The Long Read: Food Banks Have Been Busier than Ever – But There's Still Time for Change This Winter.* Available online at: www.trusselltrust.org (Accessed 08/01/21)

Chapter 7

School exclusion – just a holiday?

What can schools learn from experiences of internal and fixed-term exclusion?

Matthew Sammy

Context

School exclusions across the United Kingdom continue to be a subject of debate in the media and the focus of government policy. From my experience as teacher, senior leader and school inspector, exclusion is a delicate issue which can lead to an array of emotions for those involved. Understanding the relationships between exclusion and pupil behaviour, future life chances and the legality of exclusions are legitimate and warranted. However, such relationships are very rarely explored through the experiences of the individual who it affects the most – the child.

In this chapter, I explore the views of two brothers – Danny and Jamie – on the behavioural sanctions of internal and external school exclusion they experienced. This chapter includes the views of their mother (Sharon) as well as an assistant principal who has oversight of behaviour and welfare at the 11–16 school where the boys attend. The school is situated in a rural area with the majority of pupils being White British. Pupils eligible for Free School Meals (FSM) are considerably below the national average, and attainment and progress measures are above national averages. The school prides itself on having traditional values relating to respect for all and strong inclusivity for all pupils to succeed.

My research project had one sole aim – to discover what schools can learn from the experiences of pupils who have been excluded in order to improve school practice of behaviour management. This topic is important to all school leaders, and I hope the experiences collated in this research will be helpful when they (and other

DOI: 10.4324/9781003104698-8

stakeholders) reflect on and refine elements of practice within their own schools.

Transforming practice

As a senior leader with oversight of behaviour management, I have been involved in the processes of pupils receiving various behavioural sanctions like internal, fixed-term and permanent exclusions. In my experience, I see predominately two avenues once a pupil receives a fixed-term exclusion – i) recognition by the pupil of the seriousness of exclusion and subsequent modification of behaviour in a positive manner, or ii) further repeated exclusions which may result in permanent exclusion.

My research was inspired by one school inspection I conducted. During a meeting I had with the senior leader in charge of behaviour, she found it problematic to give me information about pupils who were excluded over the past two years. Put simply, leaders in that school did not keep a close enough eye on these pupils. There was no robust tracking of who was excluded – by ethnicity, gender or special need, or whether it was a repeated exclusion. The lack of detail given to such an important area of behaviour management did not provide this school with the tools to analyse and intervene accordingly, particularly for repeat offenders.

In the same school inspection, there was an overwhelming sense of pupils feeling their opinions were not heard about a range of issues, including behaviour. It was following this inspection that I felt convicted to investigate pupils' experiences of facing internal and fixed-term exclusion sanctions.

Frequent disruptive behaviours will impact negatively on the learning of all pupils, so exclusion introduces a 'moral dilemma' for schools and senior leaders. Is exclusion fair for the excluded pupil, or for that pupil's peer group? Creating a balance between school safety and school discipline is a challenge with significant implications. Keeping students safe and maintaining a productive learning environment remain schools' primary objectives, and some see this as achieved by removing disruptive students. I firmly believe that learning should not be impeded for other pupils. However, the reasons for disruptive behaviour can be vast, such as an unmet need, and the potential driving factors for exclusion may encompass issues such as teacher training, pupil belonging, school behavioural and exclusion policies and their application. For as Hattie *et al.* (2016: 219) state,

> As educators we must be proactive in seeking out the knowledge and skills to enable every one of our students to be successful learners. I believe that when one child fails to learn, it may have a small impact on a school, but it represents 100% failure for that child and is unacceptable.

My research aimed to use pupil voice to help transform current practice of school exclusion, offering insight for parents, teachers, school leaders and policy makers of the realities of exclusion for these students – insight that could be used to inform further debate about their own school's behavioural policy and practice.

Collecting evidence to measure impact

Evidence collection

To understand the meaning and experiences of all participants involved, I used a single-case study approach and carried out six semi-structured interviews. The use of semi-structured interviews was a deliberate choice, as these allowed participants to talk freely and enabled me to alter the order of questions depending on the course the interview took: this was important to pursue information that was not necessarily planned in the sequence of the interview process.

My study consisted of three sets of participants: 1) two brothers (Danny and Jamie); 2) the boys' mother (Sharon); and 3) an assistant principal of the boys' school. I decided to conduct two interviews with each of the brothers in order to follow up on any findings from their first interview. The order of the interviews was also deliberate, as it allowed me to gain a clear understanding as to the pupil's reality of their internal and external exclusion experiences before I spoke with their mother and assistant principal. The questions included:

To Danny and Jamie:

- Talk me through the aspects of school you like and dislike.
- How does your behavioural contract support your behaviour at school?

- How does your mentor support you at school?
- You mention your parents are 'powerless.' What makes you think this?
- Do you believe the school has treated you fairly in your various fixed-term exclusions?
- How did you feel when you received your diagnosis of ADHD?
- Did the exclusion(s) affect your relationships with teachers and if so, how?

To Sharon:

- From a parent's perspective, what are your thoughts to sanctions such as exclusion?
- Do you have any ideas of what could be a better alternative than exclusion?
- Give me examples of how the school has supported your boys with their behaviour and learning.
- How do you feel the school could have supported your boys further?
- Describe your relationship with school staff.
- What impact has exclusion had on your family?

To the assistant principal:

- Talk me through the behaviour management processes within your school.
- What support is given to pupils who are at risk of exclusion?
- How does your ethos impact your school policies, particularly pertaining to behaviour and exclusion?
- How are teachers supported to deal with students who may be challenging?

Ethics

Given the sensitivity of my research study, the ethical considerations were important to ensure no distress was caused to any participant. Each interview was conducted in a private room located in an area that ensured the participants were discussing their experiences in a relaxed environment. Pseudonyms were applied to all participants, and a full briefing about the study's purpose was provided in order to gain informed consent to take part. Within the briefing, it was made clear that participants had the right to withdraw, which was reiterated in all face-to-face meetings.

Impact

Four key themes emerged from the interviews:

- Effectiveness of exclusion
- Power
- Ethos and policy
- Special Educational Needs and Disability (SEND).

Effectiveness of exclusion

Key themes were the feeling of 'injustice' and the 'effectiveness of exclusion' as a sanction. It was evident through their comments that Danny and Jamie believed they were persistently unfairly treated, possibly because of their previous behaviour record. Being monitored on a daily behavioural report naturally heightens key students to be monitored closely in lessons, so the baggage that both boys may have carried by having a negative record could have had an impact on why Danny and Jamie felt so unfairly treated, regardless of whether the sanction was fair and warranted. I would also argue – as previous studies like Munn and Lloyd (2005) have shown – that, compared to their peers, students who are closely monitored can be sanctioned disproportionately by teachers. Munn and Lloyd also found that the vast majority of non-excluded pupils felt:

- Poor behaviour should be dealt with appropriately, whether this was detention for missed homework or exclusion for a more serious incident;
- Safety was important, so sanctions like fixed-term exclusion would be appropriate if a pupil was continually disruptive or aggressive, highlighting the seriousness of such behaviour; and
- Excluded pupils viewed exclusion as a 'holiday.'

When questioned about whether exclusion was a suitable sanction for poor behaviour, Jamie disagreed:

> If you exclude a pupil, most of the time, people like me, or somebody else, is obviously not going to say that it's fair, but

they're not going to really care about it, because they don't want to be in school anyways. I go home and get to play on my Xbox!

I, like many school leaders could question the notion of parental responsibility to ensure their child does not see an exclusion in this way, however, exclusion brings difficulties for working parents as articulated by Sharon:

> Even though Jamie might have said to you, "Well, yeah, it's a bit like a holiday. I didn't do this, and I didn't do that," me and his dad have to work. It's that simple. So, he's old enough to be left on his own. I can't say to him, "Get some revision done, get some maths done," because he just won't do it.

To consider the impact of exclusion from a parental view, Sharon indicated how little effect this sanction had on Jamie's behaviour, due to further repeated exclusions:

> I think it's [exclusion] really antiquated. Who is it punishing? It didn't punish Jamie. It didn't punish him one bit; he wasn't bothered that he wasn't coming to school for a few days. You know, he got to watch movies and play Xbox. There's got to be a better way than just kicking somebody out of school.

Power

Most school leaders would challenge Jamie's mother to take more ownership by applying suitable sanctions, such as removing electrical devices to support the punishment of exclusion. However, the concept of punishment and discipline introduces the idea of power relationships and the ultimate expression of professional power:

> My parents said you cannot argue with teachers. They tell me not to argue with teachers as I won't win. (Danny)

Danny's feelings are clear – teachers will always 'win' the argument. Interestingly, this sentiment reflects his parent's viewpoint. For me, it is not about any party 'winning.' It is about ensuring that appropriate behavioural sanctions are applied fairly and in a robust manner. Unfortunately, some pupils and parents feel *any* application of behavioural sanction is the school winning the battle of power, but in my experience, appropriate sanctions are usually applied to reinforce basic routines and expectations to help pupils learn from their mistakes in order to be successful citizens in their community.

For Jamie, whether he acknowledges or not that discipline is an inherent part of school life, an area which proves difficult for him is the communication from the headteacher, which he believes is not fair or appropriate:

> She took me to the headteacher, and he was having a go at me. And that's what annoys me, because he's the one who decides to exclude me or put me in isolation, but he never comes in and tells me himself. He always gets these people to come and tell me, but he never comes in and tells me why.

Discipline is one way in which power can be exercised. Despite the power status of Jamie's headteacher, decisions had been delegated to his colleagues to inform Jamie of his exclusion, reinforcing that teachers are always an authority, no matter what. Bottrell (2009) also argues that adults in positions of power ignore the strengths of disruptive students where there is an overemphasis on their poor behaviour, again reinforcing the concepts of injustice – a view supported here by Sharon, who felt Jamie's strengths were not appreciated:

> He's a regional boxing champ. He can discipline himself. He does hyper-focus on things. But he just can't cope with injustices. So, when he's getting told off by teachers that he's already instilled in his little brain don't like him, he feels victimized and feels picked on.

The impact of persistent behavioural sanctions for Jamie, and to some extent Danny, indicates how relationships are strained:

> My parents would be annoyed because they think I am too intelligent to be excluded. When I get in trouble, they think I am not trying my hardest and not doing as well as I should. It makes me angry that they always think they know better. (Danny)

Sharon also felt resistant to the school, questioning the relevance of her family voices being heard:

> They should be allowed to have a voice and say, actually, "I think that was a bit harsh." I've sent some emails to the headteacher and got really quite blunt, sarcastic emails back. I think, what's the point? What is the point of me fighting for these boys?

Although as leaders in education we have the power to change and influence the lives of our young people, it is critical that we use this power to 'empower' the young people we serve. I would question the way in which decisions were relayed, as clearly the information Jamie received was 'second-hand' and not from the headteacher directly. Although only the headteacher can make a decision to exclude a pupil, I feel strongly that such important decisions are relayed by the headteacher directly to the pupil. This will enable a conversation about the exclusion so that he or she can gain clarity on the justification for such a serious sanction.

Ethos and policy

School leaders would not wish pupils and their families to be resistant to their behaviour ethos; in fact, the ethos permeates the shared vision for all stakeholders with the aim of all pupils succeeding in every aspect of their schooling life. Whether or not Danny and Jamie had opportunities to express their feelings, in their view they did not, so it does indicate the need for effective communication through pupil voice. This will enable schools to be reflective in their approach to lessen the opinion of 'injustice' by the pupils they serve.

It is not uncommon for students to feel unfairly treated in certain behavioural situations. This account of Jamie indicates such an experience of one mathematics lesson:

> There are times when teachers do not always follow the policy properly; they can go straight away to C3. So, they skip stages to make it harsher.

In this instance, Jamie felt aggrieved by the lack of consistency applied by the mathematics teacher, and a subsequent issue arose between Jamie and this teacher resulting in an escalation of behaviour, with Jamie becoming verbally abusive due to these actions.

This misuse of policy is unacceptable and led to a situation which could have easily been avoided. Staff should not compromise or lower their expectations, but they should be consistent and fair in their application of policy for all pupils. Jamie felt aggrieved by the teacher's decision, and I am positive we would feel exactly the same if we were in Jamie's position. Allen and Boyle's (2018) work on 'belonging' seems very relevant here – they emphasised the importance of strong teacher-pupil relationships that understood students needed to feel they belong in a way that will give them the confidence to learn by trying, failing, succeeding and learning more.

Special Educational Needs Disability (SEND)

Staff who teach pupils who have behavioural difficulties should be equipped with necessary strategies to de-escalate potential situations of conflict as expressed by the assistant principal:

> I've given teachers lots of strategies, and I've been around; and I know they're doing them.

The confidence of the assistant principal suggests that his staff were familiar with strategies to ensure inclusion for all pupils – encompassing the school's ethos. However, it is critical that staff understand how to deal with pupils who may have additional learning needs. The reference to Attention Deficit Hyperactivity Disorder (ADHD) was a common theme within the findings of this research. Danny explained how he wasn't sure whether his teachers knew he had a diagnosis of ADHD:

> My dad makes complaints if it is something to do with my ADHD, because he is an ADHD specialist. He will make a complaint if he thinks they have not considered my condition.

Jamie's situation is different because despite having traits of ADHD, he opposed any formal diagnosis as this would prohibit a future career in the Royal Marines. Although I understand his reasoning, I would argue that appropriate support may be missed if no formal diagnosis was sought, resulting in continuing challenging behaviour at school and placing his potential career prospects into jeopardy.

It is simply inexcusable and unlawful for schools to exclude pupils without taking such SEND into account. Although Danny and Jamie's school claimed to have an ethos of inclusivity for all, I would question whether the boy's needs were fully met. As a parent, this would be of great concern, as schools have a duty to ensure the needs of all pupils are met accordingly. The 2019 Timpson Review of School Exclusion stated,

> Many parents and carers spoke about exclusion of children with SEN being the result of a failure to understand and properly identify children's needs, or using this information to put in place the right support to help them overcome barriers and engage with the curriculum offer.
>
> (p. 38)

Final reflections

Having been involved in both fixed-term and permanent exclusion as a senior leader, I do appreciate that this sanction is necessary in certain situations. However, I strongly believe too many pupils across the country are being let down by unwarranted use of exclusion – both fixed-term and permanent. As school leaders, we have the privileged role to see our young people thrive and to unlock their potential to be successful citizens within our communities. We must ensure that we are doing everything possible to avoid such a serious sanction as exclusion. You may think this is obvious – however, too often, the sanction of exclusion is used frequently with little regard to addressing the 'root cause' of issues. I also believe it is important for policy makers to draw patterns and conclusions from recent years' records to assess and analyse the effectiveness of school exclusion as a whole – to ensure pupils do not feel exclusion as unwarranted, unjustified, or even as a 'holiday.'

Recommendations

Recommendations for practice

I EFFECTIVENESS OF EXCLUSION

The effectiveness of exclusion remains a topic for debate. Jamie felt it to be a holiday, and Sharon questioned the purpose and validity of such a sanction. Schools are empowered to use exclusion when warranted. However, in order to reduce the need for exclusions, school leaders should consider:

- Barriers to a pupil's education – how are these explored in-depth with appropriate interventions to provide necessary support?
- Budgets to allocate funding for specific and effective behavioural interventions.

(see Annex 1)

2 POWER

To avoid unnecessary power relations, it is important that regular dialogue and effective communication between home and school are evident. Therefore:

- Leaders should be clear to both pupils and parents about what sanctions will be given and why such decisions are justified for the avoidance of doubt.
- Regular communication between home and school is essential – conversing, not only about the negative, but importantly, the positive aspects of a pupil's behaviour.

3 ETHOS AND POLICY

Schools are bound to the stipulations as set within law, despite possible resistance of behavioural sanctions from pupils and parents alike. Although all participants recognised the need for rules and policies, the implementation of such sanctions caused concerns to the family. Leaders therefore must:

- Embed a fair and concise behaviour policy ensuring clarity and understanding by all stakeholders.
- Ensure staff at all levels are using and applying the policy in a consistent manner.

4 SPECIAL EDUCATIONAL NEEDS AND DISABILITY (SEND)

Schools must ensure that pupils with SEND are appropriately supported according to their needs. It is therefore critical that leaders:

- Provide specialist training for staff who deal with pupils with additional needs, in order for supportive strategies to be implemented, reviewed and actioned consistently.
- Ensure strong partnerships with multi-agencies to provide necessary support for all stakeholders.

Annex 1

In order to provide necessary support to pupils, schools need a range of bespoke strategies to meet different pupils' needs. The following list is not exhaustive, but it highlights support/interventions I have found useful within my leadership of behaviour management.

Keyworker	Having a designated point of contact to act as an advocate is powerful. This can be a member of SLT, pastoral team or a member of staff identified by the pupil. Keyworkers can support pupils to develop relationships with wider colleagues to eliminate perceptions, such as 'being picked on.'
Mentoring	Pupils can benefit by talking through any issues they have with a mentor. Mentors will act as a 'listening ear' to help pupils develop their engagement and attitudes to school. Strategies will be offered, such as building resilience and confidence to give a sense of self-worth. Usually, mentors are volunteers who are independent from the pupil's school.
Daily report	Although some believe a daily report can be negative, it does allow a keyworker to praise the positives and also to intervene with teachers on any aspects which require attention.
Homework Club	The offer of additional academic support can be a huge benefit to a pupil's progress. Having staff members present to support homework will give motivation to pupils who need assistance.
Trips, visits, extra-curricular activities	Enrichment is an area that can be the 'win' to a pupil's attitude towards school. The use of school finances can be used to fund activities to allow 'disengaged pupils' to be 'engaged' in school life. I have seen this work very well, and the power of accessing these activities should not be underestimated.
Restorative justice	Pupils at times may feel they are picked on by staff. Having an opportunity for staff and pupils to discuss issues together will be helpful to bridge any conflict.
Careers advice	Some pupils have little direction in their lives. Opportunities for disengaged pupils to think of possible careers will give them goals to work towards, which may impact positively on their attitude to learning.
External involvement	Services like GP, CAMHS, Early Help, Social Care and Youth Offending will provide pupils and families with wider support to complement the care they receive in school.

Recommended reading

Allen, K., and Boyle, C. (2018) *Pathways to Belonging: Contemporary Research in School Belonging*, Leiden: Brill Sense
The editors of this book bring the importance of school belonging to the attention of school leaders for consideration in their school practice and ethos – it covers themes pertinent to those discussed in this chapter.

Department of Education (2019) *Timpson Review of School Exclusion*, London: Open Government Licence
Schools are accountable for all disciplinary measures related to exclusion. The 30 recommendations outlined in this publication provide leaders and managers the opportunity to reflect on their procedures and practice to ensure that the use of exclusions are used appropriately, and that permanent exclusion is only used as a last resort.

References

Allen, K., and Boyle, C. (2018) *Pathways to Belonging: Contemporary Research in School Belonging*, Leiden: Brill Sense

Bottrell, D. (2009) Dealing with Disadvantage: Resilience the Social Capital of Young People's Networks, *Youth and Society*, 40(4): 476–501

Department of Education (2019) *Timpson Review of School Exclusion*, London: Open Government Licence

Hattie, J., Masters, D., and Birch, K. (2016) *Visible Learning into Action: International Case Studies of Impact*, Abingdon: Routledge

Munn, P., and Lloyd, G. (2005) Exclusion and Excluded Pupils, *British Educational Research Journal*, 31(2): 205–221

Chapter 8

Schools' charity work – who benefits?

Leanne Mitchell

Context

The number of trips state schools is on the increase. Some of these trips are going further afield, out of Europe to Africa and Asia. Instead of an art trip to Italy, a geography trip to Iceland or a music tour to Austria, many schools are taking students to a totally different culture for a new experience, helping with a development project that will not only challenge them but will also support the local village or area, creating something they would not otherwise have.

Due to the rise in number of people going abroad to volunteer their services for a short time in some way, a new term has been coined: *voluntourism*. As Tiessen (2012) states, this is an alternative tourism where anyone can experience a new culture and offer services for a few weeks as part of a big adventure. Lough *et al.* (2009: 36):

> International volunteer experiences typically fall outside of normal, day-to-day routine. Theory suggests that encounters which are radically different from normal routine have the potential to change an individual's life direction.

Although much more research needs to be done into voluntourism, there is still debate over who benefits more. Project Volunteer Nepal (2017):

> Since volunteers and tourists regard poverty and misery as natural in developing countries, they put poverty and misery on a level with authenticity. For them authenticity in developing countries symbolises "the traditional" lifestyle and the lack of

DOI: 10.4324/9781003104698-9

material prosperity. Therefore, volunteers seek to work in poor facilities to make them feel useful.

While Verardi (2013) and Vodopivec and Jaffe (2011) suggest that voluntourism can be seen as detrimental or beneficial for the local community, Georgeou and McGloin argue strongly that 'volunteer tourism reinforces the dominant paradigm that the poor of developing countries require the help of affluent westerners to induce development' (2015: 403). Occhipinti (2016) agrees, suggesting that better channelling of volunteer efforts could create more 'sustained development in (the) host communities' (p. 259). So, it is important that the different organisations who create these opportunities for voluntourism are thinking strategically and ethically as to what they are offering. Do they have a long-term goal in mind that will create continued improvement and development for the host country as well as a valid experience for the traveller?

In its 2020 article 'Voluntourism: the good and bad,' World Vision (2015) suggests that one downside of voluntourism includes community resources being drained by hosting. In addition, many voluntourists are unskilled and inexperienced, and they do not spend a long enough time building up meaningful relationships. However, on the positive side, the benefits that come out of voluntourism are huge if it is well-researched, well-planned and well-skilled.

In my research I wanted to understand how the experience affected students as well as what it did for the host community. I asked myself the question as to whether these trips were justifiable, in money, in time and effort? Would it have been better to just fundraise for the community rather than students travelling out there to do the work themselves?

As an educational establishment it is important to specifically look at the effect such a trip has on our students and the difference it makes to their lives and studies, as well as the effect this visit has left on the receiving community itself. I wanted my research to help understand the deeper questions regarding school's charity work and who ultimately benefits.

Our 'voluntourism'

Our school worked in conjunction with Venture Force, who organised our accommodation, our work at an orphanage and a range of excursions. The Venture Force Foundation invited several schools out to help with the building of a new orphanage. Eugemot Orphanage is the only orphanage in the village, situated in the Volta region of Ghana, and at the time of visiting, it was home to 56 children between the ages of 18 months and 18 years, run entirely by voluntary contributions. The orphanage had been given notice to vacate the building by the end of the year as the tenant wanted it back. That is where Venture Force came in. The manager of Venture Force organised for schools to go to Ghana to help build a new orphanage, three miles from the present site: our school was one of those that went and helped to build the site.

On its website Venture Force states: 'Venture Force truly believes that all overseas projects should be relevant. Our project teams leave behind sustainable solutions to the serious worldwide issues of a lack of clean, safe drinking water and practical sanitation. Both are the cause of serious illness, death and unhappiness around the globe, issues that we take for granted' (Venture Force 2021).

In taking students abroad we should be mindful as to why we are doing it and which organisation we use in order to: a) work with other communities; and b) not negatively impact any productive good that could be achieved. I decided to carry out this research to discover how trips abroad doing charity work can affect young people, in particular when travelling to another continent with a very different culture. Our group of students went with a specific task to do (working towards building an orphanage), which made the research particularly interesting, and I hoped that this study would enable me to conclude whether trips like these were justifiable.

Transforming practice

Thirty-six students and four members of staff from our suburban secondary academy in the Midlands travelled to Ghana for 10 days to help build an orphanage. We stayed in basic accommodation in two different teams. While there, the students and the staff spent a few hours each day at the worksite mixing cement, making bricks and digging the land. There were some local workers at the site directing and working alongside the students, showing them what to do each day. This was hard physical work. It was interesting to observe how some of the physically stronger boys had less mental stamina in the heat than the smaller, physically weaker, girls. The students also spent time in a secondary school teaching a lesson, playing with the children in the orphanage, experiencing a church service, cooking with the locals, meeting the chief of the village on their arrival and exit, as well as several other excursions.

This trip was planned about 18 months before the students went on it. This gave them time to earn and save for the cost of the whole trip. Although many students were lucky enough to be given some of the money by family and friends; others used the time to earn money through sponsored events and making and selling cakes and crafts. This helped develop their independence and entrepreneurial side in having to source much of the cost themselves. It also built an excitement and anticipation towards the trip. In school, a few weeks before leaving, students spent time together team building, planning their lessons for teaching in secondary school and learning about the culture so that they were prepared, to a certain extent, for what they would experience.

All of the students took two suitcases with them to Ghana. One had their clothes and equipment in it, and the other was filled with donations of clothes and books to leave in the country for the Ghanaians in the village to use.

Collecting evidence to measure impact

Evidence collection

Adhering to BERA 2018 ethical guidance, I informed the students about the research I was doing and asked if they were happy for me to write down their quotes. They were also made aware that the questionnaires they filled in after their time in Ghana were to be included in the research. I gave them the option to withdraw from my research at any time.

On leaving for Ghana I asked the students what their expectations were of the trip and what they were looking forward to or were most worried about. While travelling and staying in Ghana I wrote down the students' views, asking specific questions about certain experiences, as well as writing down quotes as they reacted and reflected on life in Africa. Two months after returning to the UK, the students were asked to fill in a questionnaire about their experience in Ghana. Eleven of the 36 students responded to the questionnaire, which consisted of 13 questions about the student's expectations, experiences and reflections. One other student also shared impact of the experience after leaving school.

Impact

In reviewing the answers that the 11 students gave to the questionnaire as well as their general reflections throughout their time in Ghana, I focussed on four main areas:

1 Students' expectations before going out
2 Students' reflections on their experiences in Ghana
3 Students' thoughts on returning to England
4 The effect this trip had on students' life

1 Their expectations before going out were mainly based around three main themes:

- The people
  Six of the students stated that they thought the people would be warm and welcoming. Three of them thought the people would be either shy, puzzled or wouldn't like them.

- The accommodation
  The students wondered how they were going to cope with the accommodation and the food. Nine students said that they were surprised at the accommodation, with one saying: "I was expecting worse accommodation to be honest." They had been told that accommodation would be basic – with a bucket for a toilet and no sinks or showers. Although this was true for the hostel that half of the students were assigned to, the other accommodation had Western toilets and showers (which was where the quoted student stayed).

- The work
  Most of the expectation of the work (building an orphanage) was of thinking it was going to be hard, like one student explained later: "The work was tough; I probably should have prepared for that more."

2 Students' reflections on their experiences in Ghana

Towards the end of their time in Ghana, the students reflected on what they had learnt through the project. When they stated their thoughts about leaving, three of the students said that they did not want to go home, with two saying:

> I was getting increasingly sad at the thought of having to leave.

> I didn't want to leave so soon, there was much to learn. I felt that I had tackled challenges with the help of others and [learnt] what life is like in Ghana from the resident's point of view.

Some were starting to relate their thoughts to their lives back home, realising that they have it quite easy compared to young people in Ghana. Having lived alongside the poverty and experienced how the locals have few material resources, students saw that how much they have in England is excessive. Even comparing what they have in their own bedrooms to what a local owns in their whole house made the students reflect on what little a person actually needs to have in order to live:

> I take everything for granted like education, and I am moody about going to school when the people in Ghana would love to have an education.

> I realised that we don't need objects and pointless things to be happy; we need family and friends.

> What you think of as essential items at home out here you realise it's not [talking about their mobile phone].

> Even though a lot of people lived in poverty, they were very happy with their life and didn't complain about what they didn't have. I definitely took this positive attitude away with me.

Students also found themselves reflecting on what they spent their time doing. Many realised that spending hours on end on social media or gaming, often alone in their bedrooms, was not only a waste of time but also lonely:

> I waste so much time on Facebook and Twitter – I could do so many other things.

> Before I came out here, I played hours of pointless games – I could go out instead of sitting at a computer desk.

> At home I spend a lot of time alone. I like being with others here.

3   Students' thoughts on returning to England

Six of the students said that now they didn't spend their money as fast; they saved better and thought before buying something. One wrote:

> I spend more time thinking and having time to reflect on things and thinking what's worth my time and what's not. I don't spend money on trashy magazines anymore and would prefer to treat others than myself.

The students had seen another way of life different from their own. Two of them wrote about an increased confidence, and another said they appreciate how fortunate they are. They found themselves enjoying being social with a group. They understood that there was a different way to 'be' than just on social media or by themselves; there were untapped relationships that they could enjoy developing. These thoughts about their experience were changing how students felt about themselves and their surroundings:

> I'm going to appreciate everything I have, before I took everything for granted. I'm not going to do that anymore.

> I realised people ordinary like me can go on to do great things and make a real difference, and that I should make the most of everything instead of shying away and going back into a corner – that I should just be myself.

> I still spend money on myself and my family, but my time is not spent alone. I take more photos, and spend more time with my friends, because I don't want to age without enjoying my life. I write down events that are important for me, even little things, because I want to enjoy life and remember important moments.

> I feel encouraged to explore the rest of the world in greater depth. I also wish to help people who may be in an unfortunate position, so this is encouraging me to be a doctor even more.

4   How have you changed as a person through this experience?

Ten out of the 11 students answered that through this experience they are now more grateful and appreciative of what they have and the opportunities they get. Half of the students said how they were grateful for the simple things and now make the most of everything they do. The one who wrote about being much more encouraged to train as a doctor said that it was through this experience they realised they wanted to help people. Two other students reflected on what was important in life:

> Personally, I think Ghana made me realise what was truly important in life; it's not all about exam results and what you'll

end up doing in the future, because if you're too focussed on that, you forget about the time you're living in and miss out on things in the 'now' as you're thinking about later.

Ghana taught me happiness is so much more important.

One of the questions students were asked was: what were your best three moments during the whole trip? Nine students mentioned times when they were with the local community. These included:

Meeting all the locals and being accepted into the community.

Partying with the locals.

Singing, dancing, screaming and hugging at Sunday School.

Meeting amazing people at the orphanage and school and hearing all about their stories.

Having an international football match.

Seeing the children's happy faces at the orphanage when we brought them gifts.

It was evident that the whole experience of going abroad, being emersed in the culture and involved in the development project, benefitted every student. However, there was also an enormous amount of benefit to the host community. Several hundred bricks were made to help build the new orphanage, and part of the land was prepared for the foundation of one of the dormitories. The local children were also taught by the English schoolchildren, and they spent time together playing sport and quizzes.

In looking at charity work abroad it is important to ask whether the host country benefits as much as the young people. One of the Ghanaian guides working with us stated the benefits of English students working alongside them in their community:

You bring socialisation of friendship; it's also transformation. It puts a challenge to those who can't speak English to learn it. You also bring donations of books and clothes which change their lives too, especially the needy people.

Looking at the reason for the students going out in the first place, five stated that they wanted to help out in some way: "to help those less fortunate than I am by building an orphanage and hopefully making their lives a bit better."

Although over half stated this as a motivation in going, when reflecting on their time whilst out there and afterwards, only a few of the students mentioned what they had done. The trip was much more about how they had changed.

Changed lives

All 11 students said that if asked whether it is worth going on a trip like this they would definitely say "Yes." Not one student said that they were sorry to have done it, but all within their questionnaire stated how this trip had changed their life in one way or another.

Over half of the students used the word *opportunity* in their answer. They realised that this was an incredible opportunity to have been given, and they learnt many things about themselves through the experience. For some it was almost a spiritual experience where they re-evaluated their life, their possessions, how they spend their money and how they spend their time. They reflected on how their relationships with their family and friends should be the priority in their lives and how it is important to spend time cultivating those relationships and to spend less time alone. They found the Ghanaians happy, joyful and friendly towards them and enjoyed their friendship. Having time at the old orphanage playing with the orphans also gave the students the extra push at the building site to work as hard as they could in order for these children to have a completed building to move into.

The student who sent her reflections after leaving school explained the longer-term impact of the experience:

> Prior to University it was one of the only experiences I had of fully being independent, and having to take initiative, and be bold and confident enough to say 'yes' to something I may not have otherwise experienced. I definitely reflected on the trip when I moved away, remembering being scared to go away for ten days, but having the time of my life made it much easier to go away for three years and trust that everything would be fine!
>
> It definitely made a difference to my confidence. I said yes to opportunities after the trip which otherwise I might have avoided, because of fear and hesitation; for example, I went

to Borneo after Ghana, because I'd enjoyed it so much, and wanted to go on another adventure.

Ghana gave me transferable skills I wasn't even aware of until I started looking for a career; even now it opens my eyes to the ways all our experiences influence ways we approach situations. It definitely contributed to my teamworking abilities, and makes me take chances on fun, exciting opportunities when they pop up.

From my research I have learnt that the impact of volunteer experiences abroad on young people are unquantifiable. The changes that happen to an individual who is open to the experience is enormous, teaching them life skills and understanding that they would struggle to learn from elsewhere, particularly in a classroom. Giving this experience to students who are at the critical age of 14–16 years old (when they are still trying to work out who they are and how they fit in) broadens their horizons and lays before them possibilities that they had not yet had the opportunity to discover.

Lyons and Wearing (2008) suggest that volunteers who have the opportunity to mix with the local communities and take part in different activities change their whole perspective about who they are and how they fit into the wider world. If the work has been carefully selected and not laid on just for this type of westernised experience Mohamud (2013) describes:

> The developing world has become a playground for the redemption of privileged souls looking to atone for global injustices by escaping the vacuity of modernity and globalisation.

It is overall worthwhile, with individuals benefiting on a personal level in addition to the actual work they achieve in the community.

Recommendations

Recommendations for practice

1 **When leading a team** of young people going abroad to do charity work, it is important to link with a reputable organisation that has effective links with the country and an ethos of supporting a community with worthwhile work. It is also important that students are aware that they do not go out

to 'change the world' but to learn from another culture. They are not going out to 'save' someone but to learn about themselves.

Through the experiences of our young people, I would say that trips to another culture to work alongside a community can be extremely successful and also justifiable. The students developed independence as they raised money for the trip. If this money had been fundraised and given straight to the community, then perhaps it could have been used in a more effective way to support the community. However, by travelling to the country several young people developed as individuals. Their outlook on the world and of themselves changed – in a way that will hopefully affect them life, and who knows where and what they will end up doing, having had such an amazing experience and opportunity.

2 **As you prepare** for a trip like this, I would suggest that the students take time to study the culture, history and political situation in the country. They should also have an opportunity to discuss the issues that 'voluntourism' raises and their own attitudes towards Westerners going out to help in other countries. This will help them be prepared – not only with information about the weather, vaccinations and clothing, but in all of these issues – making them able to understand the trip they are going on and how to behave and think about a culture.

3 **Support students to reflect** on their learning. The trips that I have experienced through my school have not only improved the lives of the young people who participate, but they have also helped the communities through the work they have done. Ultimately both the volunteers and host community gain in some way and learn something through the experience.

Recommended reading

The Downside to 'Voluntourism' by Jessica Barrett
Farmfolio.net/articles (25 February 25 2019)
This article weighs up the pros and cons of volunteering overseas. It explores the impact on the host community and questions how useful some projects actually are. It also suggests a list of ways in making sure that the impact of voluntourists is always a positive one.

OPINION: Volunteering abroad is popular and problematic. Let's fix it. Lawrence Loh Npr.org (12 September 2019)
This article discusses the growing industry of volunteering abroad. It suggests that a comprehensive approach and a paradigm shift are needed in our thinking of voluntourism, asking specific questions before getting involved. It also includes links to articles of critiques on the experience of voluntourism from a range of international volunteers.

Voluntourism: Westerners playing saviour is dangerous to all. Kau Kauru Voices
Thejournalist.org.za/kau-kauru (27 June 2018)
This article looks at the flaws alongside the positive aspects of volunteering. An African participant in the South to North volunteering programme writes about the experience of coming to Europe. It examines the portrayal of Africa and western volunteers 'playing saviour.' It also discusses the issues that social media plays in reinforcing stereotypes about developing countries.

Voluntourism and our students: How do we avoid creating 'Barbie saviours' by C. Bailey Guthrie.
Naspa.org/blog/voluntourism-and-our-students-how-do-we-avoid-creating-barbie-saviors? (23 June 2016)
A brief article looking at the popular Instagram '@barbiesavior.' It discusses how to make voluntourism a positive and ethical experience for young people. Includes questions to ask before planning a volunteering adventure abroad.

Not every student who volunteers abroad is out to boost their CV by Sara Abbasi
Theguardian.com/education/2017/apr/04/not-every-student-voluntourist-is-out-to-boost-their-cv-international-volunteering-abroad-voluntourism (Tuesday 4th April, 2017)
This article questions the fairness of calling all volunteering abroad as voluntourism. It suggests that, when organised in the right way, many projects can be extremely effective and positive for both the community and student. It explains how social media can successfully support the communication between the hosts and those visiting, staying connected long after the project.

References

British Educational Research Association (BERA) (2018) *Ethical Guidelines for Educational Research*, London: BERA

Georgeou, N., and McGloin, C. (2015) 'Looks Good on Your CV': The Sociology of Voluntourism Recruitment in Higher Education, *Journal of Sociology*, 52(2): 403–417

Lough, B.J., McBride, A.M., and Sherraden, M.S. (2009) *Perceived Effects of International Volunteering*, Reports from Alumni (CSD Research Report 09–10). Available online at: https://csd.wustl.edu/09-10/ (Accessed 17/02/21)

Lyons, K.D., and Wearing, S. (2008) *Journeys of Discovery in Volunteer Tourism: International Case Study Perspectives*, Wallingford: CABI Publishing

Mohamud, O. (2013) *Beware the 'Voluntourists' Doing Good*, Africa on the Blog, Part of the Guardian Africa Network. Available online at: www.theguardian.com/world/2013/feb/13/ beware-voluntourists-doing-good (Accessed 17/02/21)

Occhipinti, L. (2016) Not Just Tourists: Short-term Missionaries and Voluntourism, *Human Organization*, 75(3): 258–268

Project Volunteer Nepal (2017) *Poverty Aesthetics*. Available online at: www.projectvolunteernepal.org (Accessed 17/02/21)

Tiessen, R. (2012) Motivations for Learn/Volunteer Abroad Programs: Research with Canadian Youth, *Journal of Global Citizenship & Equity Education*, 2(1): 1–21

Venture Force (2021) *Ghana*. Available online at: www.ventureforce.co.uk/ (Accessed 17/02/21)

Verardi, C. (2013) *Perceptions of Voluntourism*, Ottawa: Carleton University

Vodopivec, B., and Jaffe, R. (2011) Save the World in a Week: Volunteer Tourism, Development and Difference, *European Journal of Development Research*, 23: 111–128

World Vision (2015) *Voluntourism: The Good and the Bad*. Available online at: www.worldvision.ca (Accessed 17/02/21)

Chapter 9

Creating a whole-school curriculum

Laura Wookey

Context

I work for a Multi-Academy Trust (MAT) in the Midlands, currently consisting of 28 schools. The schools within our MAT are all primary, infant or junior schools and vary greatly in terms of their demographic and size. We have large, city-centre schools, small rural schools and everything in between – all of which have different successes and challenges. As might be expected, all our settings are at different stages of their journeys in relation to their Ofsted ratings, teaching and learning, and where they sit within their communities. Despite these differences, it was agreed as a Trust that one way to improve outcomes for all our children, regardless of their background, was to prioritise curriculum development across all of our schools.

Now, we could take the following definition of curriculum as our starting point:

> The term *curriculum* refers to the lessons and academic content taught in a school or in a specific course or program (taken from www.edglossary.org/curriculum).

However, we know that this is just the 'tip of the iceberg.' Every day, children across our Trust come to school, and the curriculum is how we fill their days. Therefore, our moral purpose was to ensure that what we provided was engaging, robust, fulfilling and meaningful – not just a checklist of content to be taught. Our Trust had the collective aim to co-construct a curriculum that would promote compassion, integrity and a pursuit of excellence so each of the children in our schools could reach their full potential and become incredible,

DOI: 10.4324/9781003104698-10

empowered individuals, prepared for the next stage of their education and wider life journey.

We knew to achieve this that our curriculum needed to be rigorous, to be progressive and to ensure retention of key knowledge and skills, whilst obviously being broad and balanced. This ambition stemmed from a Trust-wide awareness that, due to various factors including exam result pressure and national agendas, our curriculums had become narrowed. Regardless of a focus on the 'core' subjects, the attainment gap wasn't closing as we would have hoped, and we were not increasing the cultural capital of the children in our schools to the extent we would like. Consequently, as an organisation, we knew we had a moral obligation to improve outcomes for our children through developing what we hoped would be a 'top-class' curriculum. Equally, we are firm believers in the concept that 'the whole is greater than the sum of its parts,' and we knew that working collaboratively would not only increase consistency across our schools but should reduce workload for individual schools. It would afford us the opportunity to learn from and support one another, drawing upon the best practices that exist across the MAT and beyond – which is a key reason why our schools joined the Trust in the first place.

Ultimately, we were striving to create a curriculum that would:

1 Be matched directly to the needs of the children and their communities in each of our schools to increase children's cultural capital, so they could reach their potential.
2 Be progressive, meaningful and knowledge-rich, so children could make connections with prior learning and become creative, divergent thinkers.
3 Produce kind individuals who would leave a social legacy.

Transforming practice

We knew we had a large task on our hands and the decisions we made should essentially be life-changing for children in our schools. At the start of the year-long project, we brought together a small working group of 11 practitioners from across our Trust, including two headteachers, two deputy heads, two experienced teachers, two recently qualified teachers and three lead practitioners – all of whom had a passion for curriculum design. Being an outward-looking organisation, we began by researching and exploring current effective practices. This involved engaging with cognitive science research about how children learn best and visiting four primary schools across the country identified by Ofsted as having 'Outstanding' curriculums. We fed back our findings during our half-term, half-day meetings.

This research shaped our thoughts and direction, and as a consequence of our visits, reading and discussions, I produced our proposed model (see Figure 9.1). However, to ensure this was a curriculum owned and invested in by all of our practitioners, we used our whole Trust INSET day to share our findings and garner the input of all teaching staff to generate the core principles we wanted to underpin our Trust curriculum. This INSET was led by a national leading consultant in curriculum design to ensure we all heard the same messages linked to effective curriculums. By the close of the INSET, as a whole Trust we agreed that within our schools, our curriculums would:

- (Be) relevant and current;
- Empower children;
- Promote character and heart;
- (Ensure) memorable learning; and
- Provide opportunities.

The curriculum model

The curriculum model was based on an 'enquiry approach' to learning (Kahn and O'Rourke 2005). We wanted the previous concept of 'topics' to be replaced with meaningful and authentic 'enquiries' which would be driven by an enquiry question. We wanted to get away from children essentially being taught asynchronous lessons that led to them potentially retaining 'pub-quiz' style knowledge that was often not built-upon and consequently forgotten. We wanted them to be invested in purposeful learning so they could develop interconnected schemas in their long-term memories that would allow them to become creative and divergent thinkers (Weinstein *et al.* 2018). For example:

> Instead of having a topic such as WW2, we would have an enquiry which explored the question: 'Can conflict ever be justified?'. This expanded the learning opportunities for children and made their learning far more 'relevant and current.'

118 Laura Wookey

Overarching Enquiry Question for each enquiry, e.g.: 'Is it ever right to be wrong?' Launch enquiry with a hook. (This could be a memorable experience or sharing the exciting, authentic outcome so children invest in their learning.)

Maths: Progressive key knowledge and skills should be taught in this enquiry. These should be incorporated where links are meaningful, otherwise lessons should be taught discretely.

SMSC: Progressive key knowledge and skills should be integral to each enquiry. Where possible, enquiries should have social impact.

Enquiry Map: Essential knowledge and skills should be mapped out for each enquiry driver. For example: Uncover, Explore or Imagine

Foundation Subjects: Progressive key knowledge and skills should be taught in this enquiry. The philosophy should be: 'As a historian, we will...', 'As a geographer, we will...', etc. These subjects might act as the key driver of enquiries.

English: Progressive key knowledge and skills can be taught in this enquiry if meaningful links can be made. High-quality texts should be a key feature of the enquiry.

Authentic Outcome

All learning in the enquiry should lead toward an authentic outcome which will provide the children with the opportunity to reflect on and present their learning in a way that ensures it is meaningful and embedded.

Our curriculum is underpinned by the following principles. Our curriculum (is):

Relevant and Current
Our children's backgrounds and needs "along with our current culture, climate and events" determine the content of our curriculum. We use the mantra: 'Because our children we .'.

Empowers Children
Our children will develop a rich vocabulary and engage with opportunities to be aspirational, reflect on their learning, take risks, be brave, ask questions, solve problems, evaluate, develop peer critique methods and take ownership of their learning to increase their cultural capital

Promotes Character and Heart
We relentlessly focus on developing individuals who are resilient, show compassion and integrity and strive for excellence in all that they do.

Memorable Learning
Our curriculum achieves the balance of breadth and depth based on authentic, challenging learning experiences which lead to memorable learning that children can recall. It secures children with transferable knowledge they need for subsequent learning.

Provides Opportunities
Our children will be prepared for the next stage of their journeys by experiencing a set of opportunities enabling them to be well-rounded and prepared, exemplifying our 'Trust Values;'.

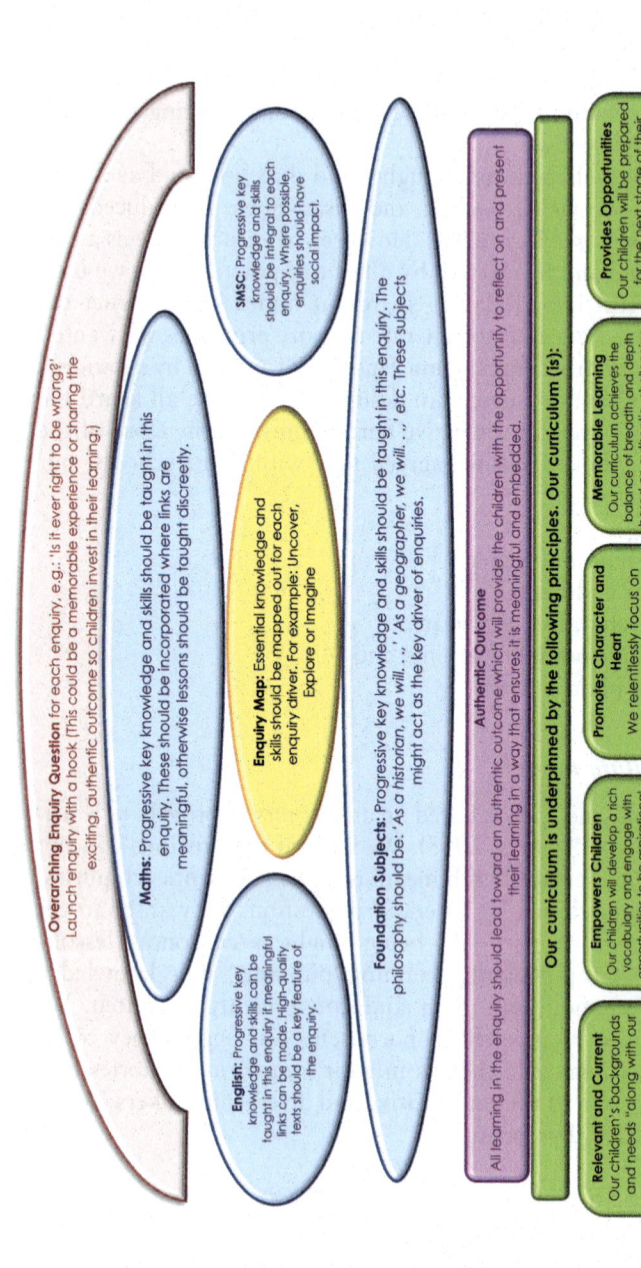

Figure 9.1 Our MAT curriculum model

Alongside learning the key knowledge connected to WW2, teachers could design learning experiences connected to other conflicts, building on previous learning from other year groups and allowing connections to be made to current global or local issues and to the children's experience themselves – like conflicts that might exist on the playground – ensuring they could connect with material that could otherwise feel quite abstract.

In line with our reading on how children retain information (Soderstrom and Bjork 2015), we wanted each enquiry to culminate in an authentic outcome where children would have the opportunity to showcase what they have learnt by demonstrating the answer to the enquiry question. Authentic outcomes could include anything from the children presenting a lecture to geography students at a secondary school; children curating a museum for the local community, demonstrating their knowledge through their exhibitions; children running a campaign linked to the theme of their enquiry; children producing interactive displays in their local doctors' surgeries, showcasing what they've learnt and providing information for the public.

In line with our principle of promoting character and heart, we wanted our enquiries to leave a social legacy. For example, an enquiry linked to deforestation might result in an authentic outcome which included children working with key figures in the local community to install additional recycling bins in the locality of the school. Another key feature of the model was the desire to draw upon and utilise experts both to share knowledge with the children and also act as critical evaluators of their learning. These experts could range from those who work in the emergency services, whilst exploring the enquiry question: 'Do all heroes wear capes?', to local farmers in an enquiry linked to the concept of sustainability.

To assist our teachers in designing enquiries, a member of the Education Improvement Team worked with one of the Trust headteachers to produce a key knowledge progression document. This took statements from the National Curriculum (NC) and mapped them across each year group for every subject, ensuring that our curriculum would be broad, balanced and progressive. This was quality assured by our curriculum consultant, and using his expertise, we designed a flow-chart to share with staff as to how to approach enquiry planning.

Throughout the development year, we scheduled three curriculum suite days – one per term – that were attended by the Trust headteachers and their curriculum leads. Here, keynote speakers shared their experiences of successful curriculum design and implementation. We also used these days to share developments and documents with our schools, giving them time to discuss how best they might proceed in terms of their own curriculum development.

Having a progressive, knowledge-rich base to our curriculum, we realised the importance of investing in all of our foundation subject-leaders in our schools and ran termly afternoon networks (one for each of the foundation subjects and science, in addition to our existing termly English and maths networks) for subject leads. These networks focussed on developing attendees as subject leaders as well as developing their subject knowledge, so in turn, they would be able to upskill the class teachers within their own schools.

It was never the expectation that all of our schools would follow the same enquiries and adopt the model exactly as presented. On the contrary, our CEO uses the mantra: 'Adopt, Adapt and Fly,' which encourages our schools to adopt the underlying principles and then adapt and innovate the model to best fit the needs of the children in their setting – the whole purpose of our model! How could we say our curriculum was meaningful and authentic if it was a blanket approach across our very different schools?

Steps to implement the model:

1 Take the statements for a year group from the NC (or key knowledge progression document) and create the long-term plan. Split these into three enquiries – one for each term.
2 Decide which subject will be the enquiry drive, which others will be incorporated in the enquiry and which will be taught discreetly.
3 Create the enquiry question.
4 Select an authentic outcome which allows children to answer the enquiry question.
5 Choose quality texts which link to the enquiry.
6 Map how English will be integrated into the enquiry.
7 Break the NC statements down into a granular learning sequence.
8 Identify the enquiry hook and opportunities to engage with experts and experiences.
9 Identify opportunities for promoting the SMSC aspect of the enquiry and the social legacy that will be left.
10 Ensure each enquiry ends with a reflection and celebration of the authentic outcome.

Collecting evidence to measure impact

Evidence collection

Having worked predominantly with headteachers and curriculum leads across this piece of work, I sought the opinion of our class teachers on their perceived success of curriculum re-design in their schools. I devised an online survey consisting of seven short questions that involved one rating matrix where teachers were asked to compare their previous curriculum to their curriculum now based on five factors and with an option to add any further comments. Three other questions enquired as to any benefits and barriers of the new curriculum with regards to themselves as practitioners and the children as learners. A fourth question asked about documents, resources and training the teachers had found useful, and a fifth asked what support they would have liked. Finally, teachers were asked to comment on what they felt was the strength of their school's curriculum and what they saw as being the school's next step.

The factors against which they were asked to compare their old with new curriculum were:

- Children's perceived motivation levels
- Children's retention levels of taught matter
- Children being more aware of the purpose behind what they were learning
- Whether children are making more links between their learning
- Whether parents have a greater understanding of what is being learnt in school.

Each curriculum lead was emailed this survey link and asked to share it with their staff, with an invitation to complete the survey to gain their opinions on the curriculum model. The email explained that the survey was anonymous and that by completing it teachers were consenting for their answers to be potentially quoted and published.

Further evidence was collected from two of our schools that underwent an Ofsted inspection following the re-design of their curriculum (referred to as School 1 and School 2); the headteachers and curriculum leads of these schools gave their permission for extracts from their reports to be shared.

Impact

As outlined previously, we knew the curriculums in our Trust schools were not fit for purpose. The attainment gaps were not being reduced enough, and knowledge was not being well retained. Ultimately, it could be argued that we were failing our children by not designing a bespoke curriculum to their needs and the needs of their community to enable them to 'fly!'

Ofsted

Clear evidence of this could be found in Ofsted reports of inspections carried out *prior* to any curriculum re-design. At School 1, inspectors stated:

> The curriculum is satisfactory, and pupils enjoy taking part in the wide range of extracurricular activities. The school is aware that there are few opportunities for the pupils to practise their literacy and numeracy skills in other subjects. Although pupils say that they enjoy the curriculum activities, these are not always matched to their needs.

Whereas at School 2, the report claimed:

> The curriculum does not provide enough opportunities for pupils to develop their learning and interests beyond the school community.

> The curriculum has been based on following commercial schemes which have not reflected the context of the school and its pupils.

Following the initial stages of their curriculum re-design, both School 1 and School 2 were re-inspected, and both reports highlighted where we were meeting our initial overall aims of creating a curriculum that would:

1 Be matched directly to the needs of the children and their communities, in each of our schools, to increase children's cultural capital so they could reach their potential.
2 Be progressive, meaningful and knowledge-rich so children could make connections with prior learning and become creative, divergent thinkers.
3 Produce kind individuals who would leave a social legacy.

Creating a whole-school curriculum 123

Inspectors in School 1 this time found:

> Leaders believe in the pupils of [School 1]. They do all they can to help pupils achieve their dreams and ambitions. Pupils are proud of their achievements and their school. They work hard and want to get even better. . . . The whole school community works together to give pupils new and enjoyable experiences. They want [School 1] to be 'The best school in the universe.'
>
> Staff want to unlock each pupil's potential. Senior leaders, together with the Trust, have transformed the quality of education that pupils receive. Pupils' achievement has never been better.

These comments support aims 1 and 3. Support for aim 2 can be found in School 2's report, where inspectors commented that:

> Leaders have made sure that topics interest pupils. Pupils remember what they have been taught. Pupils talked about history topics they learnt about last year.
>
> The Trust provides ongoing training from subject specialists. Teachers have good subject knowledge. They use this to help pupils make links and build on what they know. This is improving pupils' understanding.

Clearly, not all findings can be directly attributed to the re-design of the school's curriculums, and there is still continuous work to be done. However, the inspectors' comments do reflect a shift in focus and priorities in terms of how and what the children at these schools are taught in order to meet their needs. Equally, the latter comments about School 2 support the aim of our re-design – that children retain the knowledge they are taught and can make links with prior knowledge.

Teachers' views

Twenty-nine classroom teachers completed the survey sent out, and 28 were in a position to comment on their school's curriculum before and after redesign as shown in Table 9.1.

Our schools are all at different stages with their curriculum re-design – some at the embryonic stages – yet this feedback, although opinion-based, is encouraging and shows that we are working towards elements of our aims.

When asked of the benefits of their school's re-designed curriculum, 16 teachers commented on the engagement and motivation

Table 9.1 Survey responses

	Worse than before	No difference	Some improvement	Observable improvement
Children are more motivated with the new curriculum model.	0	1	13	14
Children are retaining more of what is taught with the new curriculum model.	0	1	16	11
Children see a clearer purpose to their learning with the new curriculum model.	0	3	8	17
Children are making more links to previous learning with the new curriculum model.	0	1	10	17
Parents have a greater understanding of what is being learnt in school with the new curriculum model.	0	10	13	4

levels of the children, along with children having ownership of their learning. Another benefit, mentioned 11 times, was how this model allows children to make links in their learning. Examples of such comments include:

> [This curriculum is] clear and focussed on the theme – striving to answer the overarching question and more systematic as a process, building knowledge like a pyramid as opposed to topic 'random clusters' of knowledge.

> Lessons overlap with one another, depending on whether we are learning a new skill or knowledge so that children already have a bank of information in their brain that they can link the new learning to.

Seven staff mentioned the documentation we had produced as being helpful to their curriculum planning, including the key knowledge progression document, with one person explaining that: "The knowledge progression documents are helpful to map out subjects that don't state year groups and give ideas."

Nine stated that the networking opportunities, the INSET and curriculum suite days had been beneficial as they were able to share ideas and best practices, whilst five commented on their in-school training, suggesting that, in these cases, the training we had provided for leads was being well disseminated back in school. For example, one respondent commented that what had been useful was: "in-house training – we have a strong teaching and learning lead, and as a school it is very clear what is expected of us." Barriers mentioned included 'time' – both in terms of planning and fitting everything into the curriculum along with subject knowledge. These are both elements that need considering in terms of leading curriculum development in a school. One respondent commented they found a barrier to be their lack of subject knowledge: "[It is] more time-consuming as [I] can't reuse planning." As a leader, staff require sufficient time to own and understand any curriculum redesign and subsequently to be able to plan for meaningful enquiries. This needs consideration and factoring into a school's curriculum-development action plan to ensure successful implementation.

Children's views

With hindsight, I wish we had sought input from children and parents at the initial stage of designing our model, as after all, one of our key aims was that our curriculums should be matched directly to the needs of the children and their communities. It seems somewhat remiss that I did not start by garnering children's thoughts on what they are taught. From this point on, I will work with leads to seek the opinion of their children about whether their school's curriculum is meeting their needs and use this to inform any next steps that need making.

Although anecdotal, some of the most pertinent feedback came from the impact the curriculum re-design has had on some of the children from one of our schools in a more challenging area:

> Under the enquiry, 'Can one child change the world?', the Year 2 children campaigned for an endangered animal to be adopted at the zoo. Despite his animal not being selected, one child was so passionate about saving the tiger that he adopted one as his birthday present. I feel this is a prime example of a curriculum that promotes 'character and heart.'

An enquiry involved Year 2 children forging connections with the residents of a care home. The children visited weekly to help them learn the key knowledge for their enquiry, and each 'buddied-up' with one of the residents. Once the enquiry had finished, one child insisted that he continue visiting his 'buddy' and has continued this into Year 4. Whilst in terms of 'providing opportunities,' the same enquiry afforded 12 of the class to visit the seaside for the first time – to say they were thrilled would be an understatement! This is exactly the evidence I need to know we are on the right track for our children!

Next steps

We still have work to do on getting our curriculum right for our children – in fact, good curriculum design is dynamic and continually evolves with the needs of our children and their community. We have identified that our next step as a Trust is to turn our model into one which is concept-based. This should allow for more authentic deep learning as, when paired with our enquiry approach, children will be able to make even further connections across and between subjects throughout their primary experience to help them make sense of their learning and give them powerful knowledge with which to think across a range of diverse contexts (Marschall and French 2018). For example:

> We may introduce the concept of tyranny to children in foundation stage when learning the names of dinosaurs in a relevant enquiry. As children progress through school, each time they encounter a tyrant or example of tyranny, whether in their English reading book, a period of history, through their RE learning, then children can continually add to this concept schema in their long-term memories. Therefore, by the time they encounter Hitler as a tyrant in upper key stage 2, they have a wealth of powerful knowledge on which they can draw to understand this significant figure from history.

Creating a curriculum fit for our children's needs is a continually evolving journey – a challenging yet very exciting one. To date, our schools should be incredibly proud of the changes they have made, as already they have led to improved experiences and outcomes (not just the 'academic ones') for all of our children. Our children only get one chance at an education, so it is our responsibility to give them the best one possible!

Recommendations

Recommendations for practice

Although this model was constructed by drawing on colleagues from across our MAT, a similar process of investigation and co-construction could be conducted within a school, with staff from across phases working collaboratively and offering differing viewpoints. I feel this approach to curriculum re-design would be just as successful within a single school setting.

Here are some recommendations for re-designing a curriculum within a school/Trust:

1 **Have clearly defined reasons for wanting change.**
   a) Where are your children currently, and where do you want them to be?

   Decide this as a whole school community. I wish I had asked schools to include pupil and parent/carer voice at this stage of curriculum design as, from the results from the staff survey, this is an area that needs developing in our schools.

   b) A great mantra to use is: 'Because our children ____ we ____' (e.g. 'Because our children have low level communication skills, we have a language-rich curriculum, providing children with plentiful and meaningful opportunities for them to become confident, articulate orators.').

2 **Establish your baseline starting point and destination.**

   Capture your baseline against which you can measure impact of future actions. This might include responses to any pre-pupil, parent and staff interviews/surveys about their views on the current curriculum provision, current attainment levels, current standards in books and any evidence that suggests the current curriculum provision is not leading to retained powerful knowledge (again, pupil interviews may be useful here). Then decide what your children need from a curriculum to achieve your ultimate outcome.

3 **Create a curriculum working group** with members from across your school/Trust. Once again, think how pupil and parents/carers may be involved.

4 **The working group should research and seek out best practice,** considering the following questions:
   a) What will our model look like?
   b) Which lessons might be taught discretely?
   c) Does this meet the needs of our children and their community?

5 **Use the research to inform the creation of an action plan,** consisting of small measurable steps:
   a) Consider the time needed to re-design curriculum units.

b) Consider timetable implications.
c) Consider how to support staff with their subject knowledge.

6   Factor in continual review points to gauge impact-to-date, reflect on actions and decide next steps.

Recommended reading

Sealy, C. (ed) (2020) *The Researched Guide to The Curriculum: An Evidence-informed Guide for Teachers*, Woodbridge: John Catt Educational

Lear, J. (2019) *The Monkey-Proof Box: Curriculum Design for Building Knowledge, Developing Creative Thinking and Promoting Independence*, Carmarthen: Independent Thinking Press

Kidd, D. (2020) *A Curriculum of Hope: As Rich in Humanity as in Knowledge*, Carmarthen: Independent Thinking Press

Myatt, M. (2018) *The Curriculum: Gallimaufry to Coherence*, Woodbridge: John Catt Educational

The first two books are written by current practitioners, reflecting on effective curriculum design in their schools with practical examples. Kidd's book brings authenticity and the human aspect to the curriculum and discusses how you can provide a knowledge-rich curriculum that meets the needs of a community. Myatt's book offers theory, research and practice to guide your thinking around coherent curriculum design.

References

Kahn, P., and O'Rourke, K. (2005) Guide to Curriculum Design: Enquiry-based Learning, *Higher Education Academy*, 30(2): 3–30

Marschall, C., and French, R. (2018) *Concept-Based Inquiry in Action: Strategies to Promote Transferable Understanding*, London: Corwin

Soderstrom, N.C., and Bjork, R.A. (2015) Learning Versus Performance: An Integrative Review, *Perspectives on Psychological Science*, 10(2): 176–199

Weinstein, Y., Sumeraci, M., with Caviglioli, O. (2018) *Understanding How We Learn: A Visual Guide*, London: Routledge

Chapter 10

How to improve outcomes for pupils with SEND

Emily Walker

Context

From analysing school performance data, our local authority (LA) recognised that a number of schools were not effectively meeting the needs of pupils with Special Educational Needs and Disabilities (SEND) between the ages of 6 and 11 (Years 2–6 in English schools). This is an issue that had also been identified by the DfE (Department for Education) and Ofsted (Office for Standards in Education, Children's Services and Skills):

> Children who have SEN and/or disabilities are part of the big picture that makes up a school; there is no division here. Academic excellence, and effective SEND provision, are all part of the same picture and a school cannot be truly outstanding if it's letting some of its pupils down.
>
> (Whittaker 2018)

Inclusion means removing the barriers that prevent children who have SEND from being fully included in *all* areas of school life: it means identifying, assessing and meeting their needs well and making sure they are achieving their potential. To address this, we designed our project to meet the following objectives:

- Improve outcomes for pupils with SEND
- Develop leadership of SEND
- Engage pupils in high-quality teaching and learning
- Make effective use of assessment, identification, monitoring and tracking
- Develop the quality of SEND processes, practice and provision.

DOI: 10.4324/9781003104698-11

At the initial project design stage, two Heads of Teaching School Alliances collaborated to create the outline and framework for delivery. Initial research into similar UK projects, combined with their own experiences of project design and delivery, led them to a SEND-specific project – developed and led by David Bartram (Prescient Education) – as the right starting point to build a sustainable and focussed approach to meet this project's objectives.

Discussions with David confirmed that real improvements could be delivered by adopting school-focussed SEND reviews, operating a triad system. In this method, three schools work together to review each other's practices and ways of working, with a view to continuing this relationship after the project had completed. As a development of earlier projects of this type, we decided to include a (preferably local) SEND Specialist Partner in the triad review process. This bought a level of rigor and expertise that would otherwise have been missing. It also enhanced the sharing of best practices and driving qualitative improvements into the outcomes, while delivering against a broader LA initiative to build relationships and improve working practices between mainstream and special schools.

For long-term sustainability, the project needed to focus on a wide range of staff, not just the Special Educational Need Co-Ordinator (SENCO), as we held the expectation that 'Everyone is a teacher of pupils with SEND.' Thirty-three primary schools took part in the project.

The project plan and training offer

The project was structured around the triad review system, with three in-school reviews (initial, mid-point, final) supported by two key training elements: core training was delivered to all participants, and then pathway training was tailored to the specific requirements of the individual schools. The plan ran over a period of 18 months with the outline shown in Figure 10.1.

Base training offer

All schools sent two staff members (whose role would be strategic in leading change in their setting) for two full days of training on

Figure 10.1

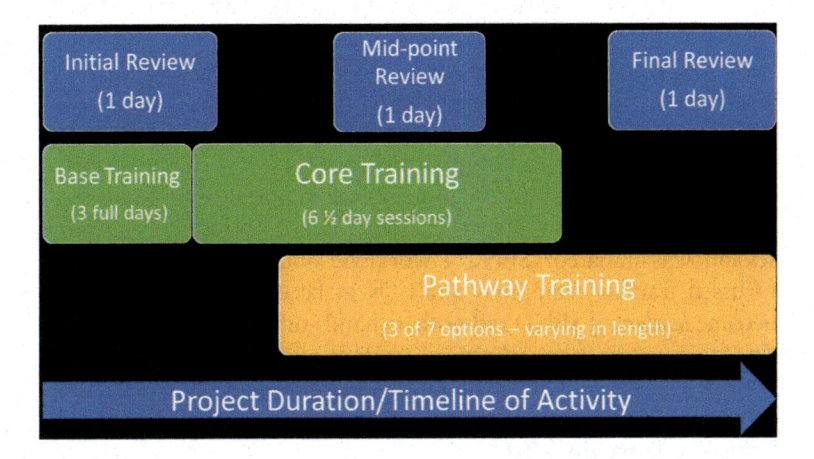

- Initial Review (1 day)
- Mid-point Review (1 day)
- Final Review (1 day)
- Base Training (3 full days)
- Core Training (6 ½ day sessions)
- Pathway Training (3 of 7 options – varying in length)
- Project Duration/Timeline of Activity

Figure 10.1 The project plan and training offer

removing barriers to learning for all pupils, especially those with SEND. The days focussed on:

1 Speech, language and communication (delivered by the LA's Speech and Language Team)
2 Curriculum offer (delivered by an experienced headteacher, recognised for developing an engaging and inclusive curriculum to remove barriers to learning)

Core training offer

All schools sent a staff member to attend six half-day training sessions delivered by a recognised specialist in the field. Schools were asked to decide which staff member would benefit most from the training and be able to disseminate the learning back in school so that their colleagues also received SEND-specific training. Initially, six areas of training were identified:

1 Graduated approach – revising the 'Plan, Do, Review' cycle of support, sharing examples of best practice
2 Specialist teaching team – approaches to use to support pupils with SEND before calling in a specialist
3 Diagnosis of specific learner needs

4   Considerations when applying for an Education Health and Care Plan (EHCP)
5   Effective analysis of data as a SENCO
6   Working with outside agencies

Potential interventions and supporting strategies were woven throughout these training sessions, reinforcing the importance of pupils with SEND receiving quality-first teaching. Later, a seventh core training session was initiated: 'SENCO workload and future practice.' This focussed training supported SENCOs to become more strategic, to become *leaders* of SEND rather than 'hands-on' managers and 'doers.' The focus was on raising the profile that 'Everyone is a teacher of pupils with SEND,' developing a shared responsibility by all members of staff.

Pathway training offer

Seven different pathway courses were identified and developed to use within this project:

1   Attendance – analysis of individual school attendance to identify trends/anomalies and strategies to re-engage pupils
2   Speech and language support for 5- to 11-year olds
3   Leadership of quality-first teaching
4   Maximising the practice of teaching assistances
5   Leading a mentally healthy school
6   Behaviour and engagement
7   Strong governance – SEND-specific

After the initial reviews, three of the seven training pathways were identified for individual schools by the Specialist Partners and the project management team, based on the review findings. It was a conscious decision at this stage to not include training around parental involvement. Although a key aspect in all education, it was felt that other areas needed to be prioritised. However, as a by-product of the training sessions, confidence improved (see Table 10.1).

Project support

Three levels of support were provided for this project:

- Project leader – I carried out this role and supported all stages of the project.

- The Project Reference Group (PRG) – this consisted of:
  - Those involved in the project on a day-to-day basis
  - Those who had designed the project
  - Representatives from the LA
  - Representatives from the Research School and external consultants who were specialists within the field of SEND.

  The PGR's role was to ensure that the project delivered the best outcomes for everyone involved through a high-challenge and high-support environment. They reviewed project data against a variety of research-based projects – and more importantly, the group's academic understanding and personal experience of SEND – ensuring that the project was on track and remained relevant and specific to the needs of participants.

- The Project Management Group (PMG) – this consisted of representatives from local teaching schools. The PMG's role was to monitor and scrutinise the project budget, to share soft data on individual schools and to understand and support any barriers the schools were facing so that personalised plans were developed to ensure all schools were successful.

With the plan built and the support organised, we launched the project.

Transforming practice: launch to final review

Launch

Before the project could start, Specialist Partners were identified and recruited to support project delivery. These were all established system leaders, recognised for their expertise in SEND: most coming from special school backgrounds. The project was then launched to headteachers and chairs of governors, detailing the project aims, roles of the school leadership team and SENCO, and explaining how they would interact with their Specialist Partners and the training on offer.

In preparation for the project starting, all Specialist Partners received half a day training from David Bartram on how to:

- Conduct a SEND review and the questions to consider
- Use national and local SEND data sets to benchmark performance and create lines of enquiry.

Following the launch event, there was an introduction to the project where headteachers and SENCOs spent a day covering the finer details of the strategy, how it would work in practice, a timeline of activity and the school's commitments for the following 18 months. They were posed questions relating to national and local SEND data in order to consider how their school compared to this – for example, how the school's percentage of pupils with SEND support, EHCPs and categories of need compared to national and local statistics. During this day, the schools:

- Met their Specialist Partners
- Met other schools in their triad – these were geographically matched to support future networking and develop a network of support
- Confirmed what was expected prior to the initial review, for example – paperwork to be completed prior to the day; a completed SEND Self-Audit to be submitted to partners before the review day; documents to be shared with Specialist Partners; a list of which staff should be engaged in the review day.

Initial review

Prior to the day of the initial review, schools had to complete an evaluation of their provision using a Self-Audit tool based on the SEND Review Guide. A school-led approach to improving provision for all' (SEND Gateway 2020). Table 10.1 gives examples of the Self-Audit statements.

Each Specialist Partner then analysed:

- The school's performance, attendance and exclusions data
- The school's SEND offer published on their website (a statutory expectation)
- The latest Ofsted inspection reports
- The evaluation provided by the school.

This focussed the Specialist Partners' questioning and lines of enquiry, enabling a rigorous review of provision on the initial

Table 10.1 Self-Audit statements

Roles and responsibilities for SEND are clear. As a result, all teachers understand and accept they are responsible for the progress of all pupils.

The school has a good understanding of how pupils with SEND achieve with individual teachers and across subjects.

School systems promote parent and carer contributions to maximise outcomes for pupils with SEND.

SEND has a high profile in staff-continued professional development and learning.

Interventions are evidence informed and coordinated effectively to ensure that a cycle of review measures the priority being addressed.

Comprehensive assessment supports accurate identification of need and informs classroom practice.

Teachers have a clear understanding of pupil need, and personalised strategies are informed by the parent-and-carer partnership. These are consistently applied throughout the school.

Progress for pupils with SEND across year groups, in a wide range of subjects, is consistently strong, and evidence in their work indicates that they achieve well.

---

review day. In addition, on the day, schools responded to set questions focusing on aspects of:

- Leadership
- Efficient use of resources
- Monitoring, tracking and evaluation
- Assessment and identification
- Working with pupils and parents
- Teaching and learning
- Developing expertise
- Improving outcomes.

They were asked to provide evidence, which resulted in many of them realising they needed to re-evaluate how they had rated themselves at the baseline Self-Audit. In one of the schools, the headteacher (previously a SENCO) completed the review from her experienced perspective: her new SENCO didn't see the school's provision in the same way and, following the initial review, understood the need to be truly reflective of the school's actual performance. Following the review, the SENCO and headteacher, together with SLT, re-evaluated the school's current provision. The confidence demonstrated was less – but more in line with the school's initial review – enabling them to write an effective action plan that led strategic change in SEND, improving the school's performance.

Following the project's initial review phase, schools were allocated a day with their Specialist Partner to write school-specific targets and linked action plans. Together, the Specialist Partners and triad groups wrote both long-term and short-term objectives for each school in the triad, establishing the measures and priorities to support SENCOs in leading the recommended development within their settings.

The short-term objectives were then reviewed half-termly with the Specialist Partners. Each Specialist Partner reported back to the project leader after these meetings, summarising what progress schools had made and any concerns they had. At this point, additional support was allocated to one of the schools who due to staffing changes was finding it challenging to implement the training they had received and achieve the targets on which they had agreed.

The initial reviews were followed up with two full days of base training. Throughout these sessions, delegates were asked to consider:

- What it would be like to be a child experiencing a day in school. What would it feel like if they couldn't understand what they were being told, how could support be given?
- What if they couldn't relate to what was being taught? How could it be brought to life for them?
- What things do we as adults take for granted? What distractions in the room can we eliminate?
- Are there resources easily available to children that would enable them to independently access the curriculum rather than relying on adult intervention, not hidden away on a tray that only support staff are allowed to access?

The schools were also offered three training pathways. SENCOs were advised who would most benefit from the different training sessions – getting the right staff member on the training was essential to ensure successful dissemination of learning back into school, so that accountability for moving practice forward was shared.

Mid-point review

At this point schools re-evaluated themselves against the initial review criteria using the Self-Audit tool, updated their data and evaluated progress made against the objectives they had written at the start of the project. Each SENCO led a review in one of their triad schools, supported by the Specialist Partner, to allow for continuity in the school-to-school improvement process. This was an important part of the project because, while we discovered that progress had been made at this point, in some cases this was not as much as expected because some of the initial Self-Audits had not been a true reflection of school practice or because a change in leadership or SENCO. Specialist Partners provided a summary of the findings and discussed with the project leader what was needed to ensure the greatest positive impact.

It became clear at this point that the SENCOs needed support in developing their roles to be more strategic, an experience that reflected the findings of the National SENCO Workload Survey (Curran et al. 2018). To provide this support, additional training was put in place, delivered by the Specialist Partners, covering:

- Leading SEND and supporting staff in their teaching (but not doing it for them)
- Refining policy and procedures
- Feeling empowered to make the changes happen.

Final review

The final reviews took place 18 months after the project launched. Specialist Partners, alongside the triad SENCOs, attended each school in their triad for a full day to compare the school's starting position to its current performance. They referred to the three Self-Audits each school completed throughout the project and investigated what changes had been made, how this was evidenced, impact on pupils within the school and the school's performance data. During this day the team conducted learning walks, work scrutiny, and pupil and stakeholder interviews amongst other activities to gauge performance.

Collecting evidence to measure impact

Evidence collection

At the start of the project, all schools and Specialist Partners signed a data-sharing/confidentiality agreement to enable all triad participants to see specified information to inform the reviews. They also agreed to confidentiality around any discussions that happened during the reviews, with explicit approval given by all whose views are shared in this chapter.

Data and evidence were captured throughout the project, consolidated, analysed and fed into the PRG. This information was based on the outcomes of the three reviews, progress made against sections of the Self-Audit and attendance at training events. It was, in the main, collected by individual schools and presented at the time intervals agreed upon at the start of the project. Data collected included:

- Performance data
- SEND performance data
- Attendance data
- Exclusions data
- Self-Audits
- School action plans, including individual reviews against project KPIs
- SEND governor monitoring visit minutes and SEND reports to the full governing body.

Analysis of data was initially the responsibility of each Specialist Partner, but as the project progressed, the analysis was done by triads. Data were further scrutinised by the PMG, experienced SEND reviewers who had led successful school improvement projects previously. They asked questions of both Specialist Partners and schools to ensure quality assurance of the review process, training and the project as a whole.

Impact

Confidence and outcomes

Table 10.2 shows that confidence levels in all schools improved dramatically. All of the data were verified by the Specialist Partners and the school leads. It was amazing to witness – but also to hear about –the changes this project had made for the schools involved,

Table 10.2 Summary of audit findings

Review aspect	Baseline review Development required	Baseline review Confidence	Final review Development required	Final review Confidence	Overall improvement in confidence from initial review to final review
Overall performance	39%	61%	11%	89%	**+28%**
Leadership	36%	64%	7%	93%	**+29%**
Efficient use of resources	45%	55%	13%	87%	**+32%**
Monitoring, tracking and evaluation	46%	54%	14%	86%	**+32%**
Assessment and identification	30%	70%	4%	96%	**+26%**
Working with pupils and parents	37%	63%	13%	87%	**+24%**
Teaching and learning	40%	60%	14%	86%	**+26%**
Developing expertise	33%	67%	5%	95%	**+28%**
Improving outcomes	48%	52%	21%	79%	**+27%**

the practitioners and their students. Two headteachers described the impact on their schools:

> Taking part in the project was instrumental in developing the provision for our children with SEND in school. Many members of staff received high-quality professional development, and the impact this training had for the school and children was remarkable. I would highly recommend other leaders to support the project in their schools to enhance and develop their current SEND provision. One of the best training provisions I have taken part in – just brilliant!

> The project has led to real outcomes, real improvements and real shifts in leadership development within our school.

SENCOs

The relationships that SENCOs developed within their triads was one of the greatest achievements of this project. They now share information, resources and advice readily with one another. They don't feel as isolated in their roles, knowing that there is someone informed who they can 'talk SEND' with, no longer being the one person who is expected to have all the answers. Many of the triads have already planned dates to complete full reviews of one another in the next academic year and interim 'keeping in touch' sessions.

SENCOs reported the project's benefits at several stages. At the mid-point review, two described the difference it had made:

> So far it has allowed us to focus on the IEP reviews and working towards ensuring we set smarter targets to make a greater impact on the children education.

> Sharpened practice, with a clearer emphasis on outcomes for children . . . Staff work together to ensure SEND provision is a priority.

After the mid-point review, one of the SENCOs talked to other local SENCOs explaining about the project. She shared the support she was receiving and identified that the project was preparing and supporting her more effectively than a SENCO qualification she had achieved previously:

> I would encourage any SENCO, new or experienced, to be part of the . . . project. It will offer you a network of support, access

to specialist professionals and a personalised programme you can follow both within the project and beyond.

As the end of the project approached, project SENCOs reported other impact:

> It has led to the SEN reviews being adapted so that they focus on showing the main area of needs, strengths of children and what home can do to help, alongside stating what the school will do to help. Upon completing the first set of reviews in Autumn, these have been further adjusted to include clear new outcomes and how home and school can support, which gives parents more involvement and allows them to give their opinions on their child's strengths and how they can support at home.

> Seeing ideas fully developed into being used school-wide and having a positive impact increases my confidence that the project will be sustainable in the future – such as change to SEND review formats and bringing in the vocabulary banks to overall increase the outcomes of pupils with SEND in writing.

> Teachers clearly understand that it is their responsibility to ensure all children with SEND are catered for and their needs met.

> SEND is a priority in our school, and I feel that everyone now recognises the complexity and range of SEND that needs to be catered for within our community.

Increased attainment and Ofsted

Unfortunately, due to COVID-19, there was no national end-of-year attainment data collected by the Department for Education in England to include in the project impact report. However, the schools involved reported that their internal data showed an improvement in outcomes for pupils with SEND, and this headteacher's experience was common to many of the project schools:

> Nationally pupils with SEND average 20% for reaching the expected standard in reading, writing and maths by the time they leave primary school. This year, whilst being a part of the . . . project, we had over 50% of pupils hitting that standard within our school.

During the life of the project some of the schools were inspected by Ofsted. Below are excerpts of the reports that demonstrate the inclusivity of the schools and the positive opportunities created for pupils with SEND.

> You are participating in a project that externally evaluates your provision for pupils with SEND, as well as peer reviews which are aiding pupils' learning. Evidence is clear that adults provide highly effective provision within an inclusive environment, successfully enabling pupils to feel supported and to flourish *(Year 1 of the project – Junior school).*

> The leader with responsibility for provision for pupils with special educational needs and/or disabilities (SEND) is experienced and effective in her role. She makes sure that pupils' additional needs are assessed and reviewed on a regular basis. As a result, pupils with SEND receive timely and effective support for their learning and welfare needs and make increasingly strong progress from their starting points *(Year 1 of the project – Primary school).*

> Pupils with SEND receive effective support from well-trained staff. This enables them to participate in lessons, alongside their peers *(Year 1 of the project – Primary school).*

> Leaders make sure that the school is highly inclusive. Pupils with special educational needs and/or disabilities (SEND) get a great deal. They receive personalised support in lessons, such as extra help from adults or adapted learning resources. Leaders want these pupils to achieve as highly as others. Pupils with SEND are fully included in school life. They love school. They particularly enjoy school clubs and musical performances *(Year 2 of the project – Junior school).*

Recommendations

Recommendations for practice

1 Leadership
- Fully immerse headteachers in the project to support the SENCO in all aspects, providing them access to the whole-school data set and prioritising SEND-focussed staff training events.

- Make the SENCO role part of the school leadership team, able to influence strategic decisions around provision within their setting.
- Use performance management opportunities to raise the profile of 'Everyone is a teacher of pupils with SEND.'
- Provide the SEND governor with SEND-specific governance training.

2   Practice and relationships

- Start by auditing your provision using one of the SEND review frameworks. This will start to identify the school's developmental needs. Invest the time to do this well, as it will enable better outcomes in the future.
- Commission a SEND review with someone who really understands SEND, who can offer high support and high challenge in a non-confrontational environment.
- Link up with other schools to conduct the reviews. The triad approach proved invaluable, and the relationships and support opportunities created between schools was an essential resource. They offered shared training, shared resources, shared knowledge and understanding of different challenges pupils and staff face.
- Establish working relationships between mainstream and special schools. There is different expertise available in each context, enabling staff and pupils to confidently access support across both settings.

Recommended reading

David Bartram (ed) (2018) *Great Expectations, leading an effective SEND strategy in school*, Woodbridge: John Catt Educational

This book will support leaders in further developing their SEND practice. It includes proven strategies from current educationalists and questions to support schools in reflection on their provision.

Whole School SEND Review Suite (2020). Available at: www.sendgateway.org.uk/resources/send-review-guide

These guides support the user in evaluating schools' SEND performances, identifying areas of strength and areas for development. They are written to allow for self-reflection, a peer-to-peer review model, or to be used by external trained reviewers. Professionals in all school can use these materials:

- Whole-school SEND Review Guide
- Demonstrating Inclusion Tool
- Effective SENCO Deployment
- Preparing for Adulthood from the Earliest Years Review Guide
- SEND Reflection Framework
- Teaching Assistant Deployment Review Guide
- MAT SEND Review Guide
- Early Years SEND Review Guide
- SEND Governance Review Guide

References

Curran, H., Molony, H., Heavey, A., and Boddison, A. (2018) *It's about Time: The Impact of SENCO Workload on the Professional and School*, Bath: Bath Spa University

SEND Review Guide (2020) *A School-led Approach to Improving Provision for All: The London Leadership Strategy, School's Partnership, Excellence*. Available online at: www.sendgateway.org.uk/resources/send-review-guide (Accessed 18/02/21)

Whittaker, N. (2018) *SEND Inspections*. Available online at: https://educationinspection.blog.gov.uk/2018/09/10/inspecting-special-educational-needs-and-disabilities-provision/ (Accessed 27/01/21)

Index

Note: Page numbers in *italics* indicate figures and those in **bold** indicate tables.

accountability, stress levels and 45
advice, headteachers, to others 21
Allen, K. 97
Anderson, D. 7
appraisal/quality assurance *see* quality assurance
Attention Deficit Hyperactivity Disorder (ADHD) 97
avoidance of harm 30

Barton, M. 18
Bartram, D. 130, 133, 143
behaviour ethos, policy and 96–97, 99
BERA *see* British Education Research Association (BERA) ethical guidelines
Berry, J. 12
bias issues 26
Bjork, R. A. 119
Bottrell, D. 95
Boyle, C. 97
Bramhall, L. 79–81; *see also* Poverty Proofing
Brighouse, T. 16
British Education Research Association (BERA) ethical guidelines 29, 30, 68, 105
British Medical Association 78
Brown, J. 7
burn-out 36

charity work 102–113; context 102–103; effect on students' life 108–111; evidence collection for 105–110; recommendations for practice 111–112; students' expectations of 106; students' reflections on 106–107; students' thoughts on returning to England 107–108; transforming practice 104–105; voluntourism 103–104
cherry-picking research 5
Children North East 77, 79, 84; *see also* Poverty Proofing
Christodoulou, D. 48, 62
Coe, R. 25
communication, headteachers and 17–18
COVID-19: beginning headship during 16, 17; first day school preparation and 13; food parcels distributed during 78; headteacher stress and 44; Poverty Proofing exercise and 87; SEND project attainment data and 141–142
CPD, headteachers and 20–21
credibility 49
Curran, H. 137
curriculum: defined 115; model 117–120, *118*

146 Index

curriculum development, whole-school 115–128; children's views of 125–126; context 115–116; curriculum model 117–120, *118*; elements of 116; evidence collection for 121; future steps for 126; impact of 122–126; Ofsted reports of 122–123; recommendations for practice 126–128; re-designing recommendations for 127–128; teachers' views of 123–125, **124**; transforming practice 116–117

Darmody, M. 43
Department for Education (DfE) 5; SEND students and 129; Workload Challenge research projects 64
DfE *see* Department for Education (DfE)
Didau, D. 48
disadvantaged children 77; *see also* Poverty Proofing

Education Improvement Team 119
effectiveness of exclusion 93–94, 98–99
enquiry approach to learning 117, 119–120
ethical guidelines: BERA 29, 30, 68; charity work 105; exclusion 92–93; least desirable schools study 29, 30
evidence-informed teaching 5–6
exclusion 89–101; behaviour ethos, policy and 96–97, 99; context 89–90; effectiveness of 93–94, 98–99; ethical considerations 92–93; evidence collection for 91–93; impact of 93–98; power relationships and 94–96, 99; recommendations for practice 98–100; SEND and 97–98, 99; support/intervention strategies 100; transforming practice 90–91
expendable income 78
experience, headteacher stress and **42**, 43

female headteacher stress **42**
free school meals (FSM) 76, 81–82, 89
French, R. 126

Georgeou, N. 103
ghost poor 76
Gibson, S. 65
Gorton, M. 8
Greany, T. 37

Hattie, J. 3, 48, 49, 62; on exclusion policies 91; 'Visible Learning Impact Cycle' 65
headteachers: communication and 17–18; energy, enthusiasm and hope for 16–17; first 100 days 11–21; leadership and 18; school-based research and 6; stress, avoiding 36–46; stressful areas of work for **38**; support network 18–19, 44–45
headteachers first 100 days 11–21; advice to others 21; communication and 17–18; context 11–12; CPD and 20–21; first day of school preparation 13–15; NPQH and 20–21; overview 12–13; perseverance and 19–20; positive outlook for 16–17; support and 18–19; transforming practice 20–21; vision delivery 15–16
headteacher stress 36–46; causes of 40–42, **41**; context 36–37; evidence collection for 39; impact results 39–43; levels by groups **42**, 42–43; levels by time of year 40; recommendations for practice 44–45; research study overview 37–38; statistical t-tests of 43–44; survey response demographics 39; thematic analysis of related literature **38**; transforming practice 37–38
Higham, R. 37
Hilary, J. 37

Index 147

human resourcing, headteacher stress and 41–42
Hutchinson, J. 8

Institute for Fiscal Studies 76

Jaffe, R. 103
Jones, G. 4, 5
The Journey map 27, 28, 29
judgements, evidence to make 54
judging the faculty footprint 54

Kahn, P. 117
Khine, M. S. 66
Kidd, D. 128

leadership, headteachers and 18
Lear, J. 128
least desirable schools study 22–34; coding system **29**; conclusion 33; context 22–23; ethical guidelines 29, 30; evidence collection for 25–26; icebreaker questions 27; impact results 30–33; The Journey map 27, **28**, 29; Midtowne schools 23–**24**; recommendations for practice 34; student perceptions of 25; transforming practice 25
Lloyd, G. 93
Lough, B. J. 102
Lyons, K. D. 111

male headteacher stress **42**
Marschall, C. 126
MAT *see* Multi-Academy Trust (MAT)
maverick leader 2
Mazzoli Smith, L. 87
McGloin, C. 103
Microsoft OneNote 49–51, 54
Midtowne schools 23; *see also* least desirable schools study; characteristics of **24**
Mitchell, L. 9
Mohamud, O. 111
Multi-Academy Trust (MAT) 36, 39; curriculum and 115–116; curriculum model *118*;

headteacher stress and **42**, 43, 44
Munn, P. 93
Myatt, M. 128

NAHT 17
National Governance Association (NGA) 18
National SENCO Workload Survey 137
Nelson, J. 4
NGA *see* National Governance Association (NGA)
NPQH, headteachers and 20–21

O'Beirne, C. 4
Occhipinti, L. 103
Office for National Statistics 78
Office for Standards in Education, Children's Services and Skills (Ofsted) 16, 23, 48, 54, 59, 115; curriculums 117, 122–123; headteacher stress and **42**, 43; Poverty Proofing schools and 86–87; SEND students and 129
Ofsted *see* Office for Standards in Education, Children's Services and Skills (Ofsted)
O'Rourke, K. 117

perseverance 19–20
planning for stressful periods 45
poverty: defined 77–78; impact of 78; Poverty Proofing and 78–79; prejudice around 77
Poverty Proofing 76–88; across Trust schools 84; actions taken 83–84; audit 79–81; context 76–77; described 78–79; evidence collection for 84–85; findings 82–83; future 87; impact of poverty 78; impacts/outcomes 85–87; poverty, defined 77–78; process issues 81–82; recommendations for practice 87–88; school, process of 79–81; transforming practice 79–84
power relationships, exclusion and 94–96, 99

Project Management Group (PMG), SEND project 133
Project Reference Group (PRG), SEND project 133
Project Volunteer Nepal 102–103
pseudo-inquiry 5
pupil premium (PP) funding 76

quality assurance 47–62; comments/photo evidence examples 51–53; context 47–48; evidence collection for 55–56; judgement evidence examples 54; learning, culture, and legacy 59–61; learning from evidence examples 55; Microsoft OneNote use for 49–51; pupil outcomes impact results 58–59; recommendations for practice 61–62; researched evidence and 2–3; research study overview 48–49; teacher impact results 56, **57**, 58; transforming practice 48–49

Raising Achievement Network 64
Reay, D. 25
research: criticism about 4; impact of 2; quality assurance and 2–3; school leaders and 3
research-active schools: headteachers' views of 6; importance 3–6; at individual school level 3–4; strategies 5–6
Research Champions 5
Roberts, A. 15

Saleh, I. M. 66
Sammy, M. 9
School Centred Initial Teacher Training (SCITT) provision 36
school preparation: first day of 13–15; least desirable schools (*see* least desirable schools study)
School Teachers' Review Body 11
SCITT *see* School Centred Initial Teacher Training provision (SCITT)
Sealy, C. 128

Self-Audit statements, SEND program 134, **135**
SEND *see* Special Educational Needs and Disability (SEND)
SEND pupils, improving outcomes for 129–144; base training offer 130–131; confidence levels 138, **139**, 140; context 129–133; core training offer 131–132; evidence collection for 138; final review 137; initial review 134–136, **135**; launch of project 133–134; mid-point review 137; Ofsted inspections 141–142; pathway training offer 132; project objectives 129; project plan 130, *131*; project support levels 132–133; recommendations for practice 142–144; Self-Audit statements 134, **135**; SENCOs relationships 140–141; transforming practice 133–137
Sherrington, T. 48
Sinner, P. 26
Smyth, E. 43
Social Mobility Commission 76
Soderstrom, N. C. 119
Special Educational Need Co-Ordinator (SENCO) 130, 135–137, 140–141
Special Educational Needs and Disability (SEND) 97–98, 99; improving outcomes for pupils with (*see* SEND pupils, improving outcomes for)
Stewart, D. S. 7
stress *see* headteacher stress
stressful headteachers work areas **38**
support network 18–19; headteachers, stress and 44–45
Sustain 78

Teaching School Alliance (TSA) 36, 39
Tiessen, R. 102
time of year headteachers stress levels 40

Timpson Review of School Exclusion 98
Todd, L. 87
triangulation 49, 54
Trussell Trust 78, 84, 86, 115–116; INSET 117
TSA *see* Teaching School Alliance (TSA)

Venture Force Foundation 103–104
Verardi, C. 103
'Visible Learning Impact Cycle' (Hattie) 65
vision delivery, headship 15–16
Vodopivec, B. 103
voluntourism 102, 103–104; *see also* charity work
'Voluntourism: the good and bad' (World Vision) 103

Walker, E. 9
Wardle, C. 8
Wearing, S. 111
Weinstein, Y. 117

Whittaker, N. 129
whole-school research 64–74; children's interviews 71; conclusions 71–72; context 64–65; evidence collection for 67–68; focus group, teachers' views 70; impact on children 70; journals, teachers' views 69; on marking issues 65–66; new approaches to 66–67; recommendations for practice 72–74; teacher involvement in 66; teachers' views 68–69; transforming practice 65; workload impact 68
Whole School SEND Review Suite 143
Willingham, D. 62
Woods, P. 15
Wookey, L. 9
work/life balance 18
World Vision 103

YouGov survey 78

Taylor & Francis eBooks

www.taylorfrancis.com

A single destination for eBooks from Taylor & Francis with increased functionality and an improved user experience to meet the needs of our customers.

90,000+ eBooks of award-winning academic content in Humanities, Social Science, Science, Technology, Engineering, and Medical written by a global network of editors and authors.

TAYLOR & FRANCIS EBOOKS OFFERS:

- A streamlined experience for our library customers
- A single point of discovery for all of our eBook content
- Improved search and discovery of content at both book and chapter level

REQUEST A FREE TRIAL
support@taylorfrancis.com

Routledge
Taylor & Francis Group

CRC Press
Taylor & Francis Group